Que®

System 7 Quick Reference

Deirdre Maloy

System 7 Quick Reference.

Copyright ©1992 by Que Corporation.

All rights reserved. Printed in the United States of America. No part of this book may be used or reproduced in any form or by any means, or stored in a database or retrieval system, without prior written permission of the publisher except in the case of brief quotations embodied in critical articles and reviews. Making copies of any part of this book for any purpose other than your own personal use is a violation of United States copyright laws. For information, address Que Corporation, 11711 North College Avenue, Suite 140, Carmel, IN 46032.

Library of Congress Catalog Number: 91-67192

ISBN: 0-88022-835-0

This book is sold *as is*, without warranty of any kind, either express or implied, respecting the contents of this book, including but not limited to implied warranties for the book's quality, performance, merchantability, or fitness for any particular purpose. Neither Que Corporation nor its dealers or distributors shall be liable to the purchaser or any other person or entity with respect to any liability, loss, or damage caused or alleged to be caused directly or indirectly by this book.

95 94 93 92 91   4 3 2 1

Interpretation of the printing code: the rightmost double-digit number is the year of the book's printing; the rightmost single-digit number is the number of the book's printing. For example, a printing code of 91-1 shows that the first printing of the book occurred in 1991.

This book is based on Apple System 7.

Que Quick Reference Series

The *Que Quick Reference Series* is a portable resource of essential microcomputer knowledge. Drawing on the experience of many of Que's best-selling authors, this series helps you easily access important program information. The *Que Quick Reference Series* includes these titles:

1-2-3 for DOS Release 2.3 Quick Reference
1-2-3 for DOS Release 3.1+ Quick Reference
1-2-3 for Windows Quick Reference
1-2-3 Release 2.2 Quick Reference
Allways Quick Reference
AutoCAD Quick Reference, 2nd Edition
Batch Files and Macros Quick Reference
CheckFree Quick Reference
CorelDRAW! Quick Reference
dBASE IV Quick Reference
Excel for Windows Quick Reference
Fastback Quick Reference
Hard Disk Quick Reference
Harvard Graphics Quick Reference
LapLink Quick Reference
Microsoft Word 5 Quick Reference
Microsoft Word Quick Reference
Microsoft Works Quick Reference
MS-DOS 5 Quick Reference
MS-DOS Quick Reference
Norton Utilities Quick Reference
Paradox 3.5 Quick Reference
PC Tools 7 Quick Reference
Q&A 4 Quick Reference
QuarkXPress 3.1 Quick Reference
Quattro Pro Quick Reference
Quicken Quick Reference
System 7 Quick Reference
UNIX Programmer's Quick Reference
UNIX Shell Commands Quick Reference
Windows 3 Quick Reference
WordPerfect 5.1 Quick Reference
WordPerfect for Windows Quick Reference
WordPerfect Quick Reference

Publisher

Lloyd J. Short

Series Director

Karen A. Bluestein

Production Editor

Laura J. Wirthlin

Technical Editor

Mark Andrews

Production Team

Brad Chinn, Sandy Grieshop, Betty Kish, Anne Owen, Joe Ramon, John Sleeva

Trademark Acknowledgments

Apple, AppleShare, AppleTalk, EtherTalk, ImageWriter, LaserWriter, LocalTalk, Mac, Macintosh, MultiFinder, StyleWriter, and TokenTalk are registered trademarks and Balloon Help, Finder, and TrueType are trademarks of Apple Computer, Inc. Classic is a registered trademark licensed to Apple Computer, Inc. Berkeley and After Dark are trademarks of Berkeley Systems. Claris, MacDraw, MacPaint, MacProject, and MacWrite are registered trademarks and Resolve is a trademark of Claris Corporation. HyperCard is a registered trademark of Apple Computer, Inc. licensed to Claris Corporation. Farallon is a trademark and MacRecorder and PhoneNet are registered trademarks of Farallon Computing, Inc. Fastback is a registered trademark of Fifth Generation Systems, Inc. Microsoft, Microsoft Excel, Microsoft Windows, and Microsoft Word are registered trademarks of Microsoft Corporation. NuBus is a trademark of Texas Instruments, Inc. PostScript is a registered trademark of Adobe Systems, Incorporated. Redux is a trademark of Microseeds, Inc. SUM Tools is a registered trademark of Symantec Corporation. TOPS is a registered trademark of Centram Systems West, Inc.

Table of Contents

Introduction

System 7 Quick Reference is not a rehash of traditional documentation. Instead, this book is a guide to the new and updated features of System 7.

For new Macintosh users, the first section briefly explains basic Macintosh concepts and terms. The next section describes System 7's new features, equipment requirements, and installation procedures.

The Command Reference provides an alphabetical listing of the new and updated features of System 7. Each entry includes the purpose of the feature and instructions for its use. Some entries also include tips and precautions and references to related entries.

System 7 Quick Reference also includes a guide to the items on the Finder's menus, a list of common keyboard shortcuts, and a glossary of key Macintosh and System 7 terms.

Now you have essential information at your fingertips with *System 7 Quick Reference*—and the entire *Que Quick Reference Series*.

HINTS FOR USING THIS BOOK

System 7 Quick Reference is a guide to the new and updated features of System 7. For quick reference, this book is organized in six sections:

- The first section, Macintosh Basics, briefly explains basic Macintosh concepts and terms.

- The Getting Started with System 7 section describes System 7's new features, equipment requirements, and installation procedures.

- The Command Reference alphabetically lists the new and updated features of System 7 and provides step-by-step instructions for using each feature.

- The Finder Menu Reference lists all Finder menus and directs you to the related Command Reference entries.

- The Keyboard Shortcuts section lists common Command (⌘) key shortcuts.

- The Glossary defines Macintosh and System 7 terms and provides references to related Command Reference entries.

For more complete information on other features of your Macintosh, ask your book dealer for *The Big Mac Book*, *The Little Mac Book*, or *Using the Macintosh with System 7*, all published by Que.

Conventions used in this book

As you read this book, keep in mind the following conventions:

- The keys you press and text you type appear in boldface blue type. In this book, the text you type appears in UPPERCASE, but you can use upper- or lowercase.

- To use key combinations, hold down the first key, such as the Shift or Command (⌘) key, as you press the second key. The following is a typical entry:

    You also can press ⌘-X.

- All on-screen messages appear in a `special` typeface. The following is a typical entry:

  Your Macintosh displays

  ```
  Welcome to Macintosh
  ```

- The information in this book is extensively cross-referenced. For more information about a feature, turn to the section or topic referenced in *italic* type. The following is a typical entry:

  See also *System Folder.*

MACINTOSH BASICS

This section provides information that new Macintosh users need in order to use the rest of this book. If you already understand the basic techniques for using a Macintosh computer, you can skip this section.

Each Macintosh includes software that teaches you how to use a Macintosh computer—either a Guided Tour or Macintosh Basics. These programs provide an excellent way to learn and practice the fundamentals described in this section.

Mouse Basics

The mouse enables you to point to and select various items on-screen. When you move the mouse across a flat surface, the Macintosh translates your movements to the mouse pointer on-screen. The mouse is velocity-sensitive: the faster you move the mouse, the farther the computer moves the mouse pointer.

To point

Move the mouse across a flat surface (such as a mouse pad) until the mouse pointer is over the item to which you want to point.

To click

Point to (move the mouse pointer over) an item and then press and release the mouse button.

When you click an icon, you select that icon. When you click an item in a window, the effect depends on the type of item you clicked; for more information, see *Windows* later in this section.

To deselect an item, click anywhere else on-screen.

To Shift-click

Click an item, and then hold down the Shift key as you click the second (and subsequent) items.

When you Shift-click items, you select all the items.

To deselect all the selected items, release the Shift key and click anywhere else on-screen. To deselect a selected item without deselecting all the selected items, Shift-click that item again.

To double-click

Click (press and release the mouse button) an item twice in rapid succession.

When you double-click an icon, you open that file. This technique is equivalent to clicking the icon and selecting the Open command from the File menu.

To drag

Hold down the mouse button and move the mouse across a flat surface (such as a mouse pad).

The item you are dragging moves on-screen.

To reposition an icon, drag the icon itself. To reposition a window, drag its title bar (the striped bar at the top of the window).

If you run out of room to drag the mouse, lift the mouse from the surface and reposition it where you have more room (such as in the center of the mouse pad).

When you move a mouse without sliding it across a flat surface, the mouse pointer does not move.

To use a selection rectangle

Click at one edge of the area containing the items you want to select, and then drag the mouse to select (highlight) all the items.

To deselect selected items or to select additional items after you release the mouse button, you can Shift-click those items.

Menus

A menu is a list of related commands (actions your computer can perform). The menu names appear in the *menu bar* at the top of the screen.

To select a menu

Click the menu name that appears in the menu bar at the top of the screen.

To select a command from a menu

1. Select the menu.

2. Drag the mouse to highlight the command you want to select.

3. Release the mouse button.

To use the Help menu

The first menu you should select is the Help menu, located at the right end of the menu bar.

1. Click the picture of the question mark.

   System 7 displays the Help menu.

2. Drag the mouse to highlight the Show Balloons command.

3. Release the mouse button.

   This action selects the Show Balloons command.

For more information on the Help menu, see *Help Menu* in the Command Reference.

For information on other Finder menus, see the Finder Menu Reference section.

Windows

Windows consist of the following basic parts; however, not all windows have all features.

Title bar

The title bar is the striped bar at the top of the window (where the title of the window appears).

To move a window, click anywhere in the title bar and drag the window to a different location.

Close box

The close box is the small box in the upper left corner of the window (at the left end of the title bar).

To close a window, click the close box.

Zoom box

The zoom box is the box within a box in the upper right corner of a window (at the right end of the title bar).

To reduce or enlarge a window, click the zoom box.

To set the sizes between which the zoom box zooms, use the size box.

Scroll bars

Scroll bars are the gray bars at the right or bottom (or both) of some windows. Scroll bars appear whenever the window contains more items than you can view on-screen at one time.

Scroll arrows appear at both ends of the scroll bars, and a *thumb* (a square box that indicates your relative position in the window's contents) appears somewhere along the length of each scroll bar.

To scroll a window, you can use any of the following techniques:

- Click one of the scroll arrows.

  System 7 scrolls the window's view in the direction of the arrow.

- Click in the gray bar.

  Clicking a vertical scroll bar above the thumb moves the window's view up one screen; clicking below the thumb moves the window's view down one screen.

  Clicking a horizontal scroll bar to the right of the thumb moves the window's view right one screen; clicking to the left of the thumb moves the window's view left one screen.

- Drag the thumb to the new (relative) position.

Size box

The size box is the box within a box in the lower right corner of the window (between the scroll arrows).

To resize the window, click and drag the size box in the appropriate direction.

GETTING STARTED WITH SYSTEM 7

This section describes new features of System 7, equipment requirements for using System 7, and procedures for installing System 7.

New Features

System 7 includes the following new features. For information about using these features, see the referenced entry in the Command Reference.

- You can run more than one program at one time; previously, this feature was available only when you selected MultiFinder. (With System 7, the Finder incorporates the features of MultiFinder.)

- You can switch between programs by using the Application menu. See *Application Menu*.

- You can automatically update documents with information from other documents (even in another application or on another computer on the network) whenever you modify the source documents. See *Automatic Updating*.

- You can share files between Macintoshes on the same network without additional software. See *File Sharing*.

- You can locate files by name, date modified, size, kind, or comment by using the Find command on the Finder's File menu. See *Find Command*.

- You can see the contents of more than one folder (and of folders within folders) at one time by using outline views. See *Finder*.

- You can get on-line help from within applications. See *Help Menu*.

- You can use custom icons for documents and applications. See *Icons*.

- You can create labels with custom text and colors and assign the labels to icons. See *Labels Control Panel*.

- You must select the Empty Trash command to empty the Trash. See *Trash*.

- The System Folder contains several smaller folders. See *Apple Menu Items Folder*, *Control Panels Folder*, *Extensions Folder*, *Preferences Folder*, and *Startup Items Folder*.

- Desk accessories no longer appear only on the Apple menu, and you can open a desk accessory by double-clicking its icon. See *Desk Accessories*.

- TrueType makes fonts appear correctly in any type size. See *TrueType Fonts*.

Equipment Requirements

To run System 7 effectively, your Macintosh should have at least 4 megabytes of RAM. If your Macintosh has only 2 megabytes of RAM, you can install System 7, but you may experience the following problems:

- Your Macintosh displays memory warnings when you use most applications.

- The Finder repeatedly asks to close all its windows (because the Macintosh does not have enough memory to keep them open) when you are using an application.

- Some applications enable you to work on-screen, but your Macintosh does not have enough memory to save the document.

- Documents print slowly or not at all.

- Although you installed only TrueType fonts, the Macintosh uses the old scaled (and jagged) fonts— or a font other than the font you selected.

These problems do not occur if your Macintosh has enough RAM. If you use only very small applications, you may find that 2.5 megabytes is sufficient. If you want to use File Sharing, 4 megabytes is the minimum.

You also need a hard disk. For temporary purposes, you can install and use System 7 from a high-density (1.44M) floppy disk, but for optimal speed (and to take advantage of features such as File Sharing) you must install System 7 on a hard disk.

Your Macintosh must be a Plus, SE, Classic, LC, or II. System 7 does not run on 128K, 512K or 512KE models.

Before You Install System 7

Some of your applications and utilities may be incompatible with System 7. Before you install System 7 on your hard disk, check for potential compatibility problems.

To check for compatibility problems

1. If you have not already installed HyperCard 1.2.2 (or a later version) on your hard disk, copy it from the HyperCard disks included in your System 7 upgrade kit.

2. Copy the Before You Install System 7 and Compatibility Checker HyperCard stacks from the Before You Install System 7 disk included in your System 7 upgrade kit.

3. Double-click the Before You Install System 7 icon.

4. To learn more about System 7's new features, click What's New in System 7.

5. To enter the Compatibility Checker, click Compatibility Checker.

6. In the Compatibility Checker window, click the Start Checking button.

The Compatibility Checker checks the items on your hard disk against a library provided by hundreds of software developers and evaluates what items work with System 7, what items may have problems, and what items are incompatible.

If the Compatibility Checker finds incompatible or questionable items in the System Folder, it alerts you with the following message:

```
Attention: Potential Problems With
System Folder Items.
```

Having incompatible or questionable items in your System Folder can prevent System 7 from starting or running smoothly.

7. Click the Move Items button to move incompatible System Folder items.

The Compatibility Checker creates a May Not Work With System 7 folder and moves all the offending items to this new folder.

System 7 then displays the Compatibility Report. This report classifies programs as Not available, Must upgrade, Mostly compatible, or Compatible.

Please note that the Compatibility Checker is extremely finicky—the offending System Folder items may work properly on your Macintosh. For now, however, move these items out of your System Folder. Later, you can follow the steps in the *Extensions Folder* entry (in the Command Reference) to determine whether these items work with your new System Software.

8. Examine the Compatibility Report. Click the Print Report button to print the report or click the Save Report button to save the report to a file on disk.

9. Take action on the compatibility report:

Category	*Action*
Not available	You can install System 7, but use these items with caution. If possible, contact the software publisher for additional information on compatibility.
	If you need to use a program that is not System 7 compatible, you can run multiple System versions. See *Using Multiple System Versions on One Macintosh* later in this section.
Must upgrade	You can install System 7, but you should upgrade to a compatible version of these programs before using them with System 7. Contact the software publisher for additional information on compatibility.
	If you need to use a program that is not System 7 compatible, you can run multiple System versions. See *Using Multiple System Versions on One Macintosh* later in this section.
Mostly compatible	You do not need to do anything about these items except upgrade to a fully compatible version of the program when one is available. If these programs are incompatible with a System 7 feature, such as 32-bit addressing or virtual memory, disable that feature before using the program.
Compatible	The program's developer has informed Apple that the program is fully compatible with System 7. You can use the items in this category with confidence (although this label does not necessarily mean that the program takes advantage of System 7's new features).

Back Up Your Hard Disk

Back up your hard disk before you install System 7. The best method is to use a commercial backup utility such as Fastback or Redux.

If you do not use a commercial backup utility, copy all your important files onto floppy disks, another hard disk, or other removable media. Backing up your hard disk ensures you will not lose any important files when you install System 7.

In addition to backing up your hard disk, many developers strongly recommend that you use the following procedure for optimal installation of System 7.

To install System 7 optimally

1. Make *two* backups of your hard drive.

2. Reformat your hard drive, preferably with new drivers. Silverlining from LaCie has excellent utilities.

    If you have a program such as SUM Tools, you can check your hard disk for bad sectors after you initialize it (but before you install System 7) and lock those sectors.

3. Install System 7 using the Installer. See *Using the Installer*.

4. Copy files from your backup. Be sure not to replace the new System 7 files with your old System's files.

This installation method is time-consuming and can be aggravating, but it is the cleanest way to install System 7.

To preserve file comments

The Desktop file is an invisible file on your hard disk where the Finder stores information (such as icons and file comments) about how your files appear on the

Desktop. From time to time, the Finder may rebuild this file, usually after displaying the following message:

`Hard disk 40 needs minor repairs.`

When rebuilding the Desktop, the Finder updates the icons in the new Desktop file and removes any file comments.

System 7's first act is to rebuild your Desktop, thus removing any file comments you typed in Get Info boxes. If you have extensive file comments and want to preserve them, follow these steps:

1. Copy files with comments to floppy disks. (Unfortunately, you cannot use System 7's Find command to find files with comments.)

2. Install System 7 using the Installer. See *Using the Installer*.

3. Copy the files from the floppy disks back to your hard disk.

   System 7 rebuilds the Desktop only on media larger than a high-density floppy disk, so when you reload your files from floppy disks, System 7 leaves your file comments intact.

Using the Installer

The Installer's purpose is to update System versions easily and quickly. (Installing System 7's eight disks would be quite complicated without an installation program.)

To install System 7 with the recommended configuration

1. From the File menu, select Shut Down.

2. Insert the Installer 1 disk into your computer.

3. Turn on your Macintosh.

4. After the Macintosh starts, double-click the Install document's icon.

   The Installer recommends a configuration based on your hardware configuration.

   To install options other than those listed in the Installer window, you must customize the installation (see the following set of steps).

5. Make sure that the drive that appears on-screen is the one where you want to install System 7. If not, click the Switch Disk button until the correct drive appears.

6. To install the recommended configuration, click the Install button.

   Follow the Installer's instructions for inserting the other disks.

7. When the Installer reports successful installation, click the Quit button.

8. If you want to continue working, click the Restart button; otherwise, click the Shut Down button.

To install System 7 with a custom configuration

1. From the File menu, select Shut Down.

2. Insert the Installer 1 disk into your computer.

3. Turn on your Macintosh.

4. After the Macintosh starts, double-click the Install document's icon.

   The Installer recommends a configuration based on your hardware configuration.

   To install options other than those listed in the Installer window, you must customize the installation.

5. Make sure that the drive that appears on-screen is the one where you want to install System 7. If not, click the Switch Disk button until the correct drive appears.

6. To install a custom configuration, click the Customize button.

   The Installer lists the items you can install.

7. Select the items you want to install by clicking the first item and Shift-clicking subsequent items.

   If you click only one item at a time, information about that item, including its installed size, appears at the bottom of the screen.

8. Click the Install button. Follow the Installer's instructions for inserting the other disks.

9. When the Installer reports successful installation, click the Quit button.

10. If you want to continue working, click the Restart button; otherwise, click the Shut Down button.

To conserve disk space

After installing System 7 (particularly if you use the recommended installation), check the contents of your System Folder to make sure that you are not wasting disk space.

To leave more room on your hard disk for applications and documents, delete all unneeded files from within your System Folder:

- Desk accessories you don't use. Initially, System 7 stores desk accessory files in the Apple Menu Items folder (in the System Folder), but you can store them anywhere (except the Trash).

- Printer drivers for printers you don't have on your system. System 7 stores printer driver files in the Extensions folder (in the System Folder).

- Fonts you don't use. To see which fonts are installed, double-click the System file icon.

- Sounds you don't use. To see which sounds are installed, double-click the System file icon.

Do not throw away an item if you are unsure whether you use it.

Caution

System 7 stores only fonts, sounds, and keyboard layouts in the System file itself. The Installer removes incompatible sounds, fonts, and keyboard layouts and replaces them with System 7 versions. (Note that System 7 installs TrueType versions of fonts, if they are available.) The Installer also moves desk accessories outside the System file.

Available Features by Macintosh Model

The following is a list of Macintosh models and the System 7 memory options they support. For more information, see *Memory Control Panel* in the Command Reference.

Model	Virtual Memory	32-bit Addressing
Macintosh Classic	no	no
Macintosh LC	no	no
Macintosh IIsi	yes	yes
Macintosh IIci	yes	yes
Macintosh IIfx	yes	yes
Macintosh Plus	no	no
Macintosh SE	no	no
Macintosh SE/30	yes	yes*
Macintosh II, no PMMU	no	no
Macintosh II with PMMU	yes	yes*
Macintosh IIx	yes	yes*
Macintosh IIcx	yes	yes*

* With Connectrix's Mode 32 software (distributed free by Apple).

Using Multiple System Versions on One Macintosh

If you (or some of your software packages) are not ready to take the full plunge into System 7, you can install multiple System versions. This technique is recommended for advanced users only.

To use multiple System versions with two hard disks

1. Leave the previous System on one hard disk and upgrade to System 7 on the other. For more information, see *Using the Installer*.

2. Use the Installer's Customize option to update the printer drivers of the older System to those from System 7. For more information, see *Using the Installer*.

3. Use the Startup Device Control Panel to select the hard drive from which you want to start your Macintosh. (Select the hard drive that holds the System you want to use.)

To use multiple System versions with one hard disk

This method is complex and requires great care. If you mix up the Systems, the computer may not start.

1. Before installing System 7, make a copy of the System Folder. Name it Sys 6 System.

2. Make a new folder and name it Sys 6 Finder.

3. Move the Finder file from the Sys 6 System folder to the Sys 6 Finder folder.

4. Review the Sys 6 System folder and remove all non-Apple items (PostScript fonts, preferences files, and so on). These items remain in the original System Folder. Also remove any printer drivers.

5. Install System 7. For more information, see *Using the Installer*.

6. Make a new folder and name it Sys 7 Finder.

7. Copy the Finder file from the System Folder to the Sys 7 Finder folder (hold down the Option key and drag the icon).

8. Make a new folder and name it Sys 7 System.

9. Copy the Apple items (refer to step 4) from the System Folder and put them in the Sys 7 System folder.

10. To change from System 7 to System 6, copy the contents of the Sys 6 System folder and the Sys 6 Finder folder to the System Folder.

   To change from System 6 to System 7, copy the contents of the Sys 7 System folder and the Sys 7 Finder folder to the System Folder.

Using Multiple System Versions on One Network

To use multiple System versions on one network, update all non-System 7 Macintoshes with the System 7 printer drivers for each shared printer. With this one exception, the System version on each computer does not affect the other computers on the network.

COMMAND REFERENCE

This Command Reference is an alphabetical listing of the new and updated features of System 7. Each entry includes the purpose of the feature and instructions for its use. Some entries also include tips and precautions and references to related entries.

Access Privileges

Purpose

Enables you, as the *owner* of a folder or disk, to control which network users can see, use, or modify the disks, folders, or files you own. Unless you specifically grant permission, no one else on the network has access to your files.

You can own files and folders on other computers, and you can enable others to store folders and files they own on your computer.

You assign access privileges on networks only.

To review and set privileges for shared folders and disks

1. Highlight the item you want to review or for which you want to set access privileges. This item can be a program, document, folder, or disk.

2. From the File menu, select Sharing.

   System 7 displays a dialog box.

3. Select none, any, or all of the check boxes for Owner:

Check box	*Effect*
See folders	Enables the owner to see folders within the published folder or volume when accessing your computer from another computer.
See files	Enables the owner to see the files within the published folder or volume when accessing your computer from another computer.
Make changes	Enables the owner to make changes to the items within the published folder or volume (including adding new items or deleting existing items) when accessing your computer from another computer.

4. From the User/Group pop-up menu, select a user or group to whom you want to assign special access privileges. (You define users and groups in the Users & Groups Control Panel.)

5. Select none, any, or all of the check boxes for this user or group:

Check box	*Effect*
See folders	Enables the user or group to see folders within the published folder or volume when accessing your computer from another computer.
See files	Enables the user or group to see the files within the published folder or volume when accessing your computer from another computer.
Make changes	Enables the user or group to make changes to the items within the published folder or volume (including adding new items or deleting existing items) when accessing your computer from another computer.

6. The last set of check boxes affects users other than the owner (you) or the specified user or group. Select none, any, or all of the check boxes for Everyone:

Check box	*Effect*
See folders	Enables everyone to see folders within the published folder or volume when accessing your computer from another computer.
See files	Enables everyone to see the files within the published folder or volume when accessing your computer from another computer.

Check box	*Effect*
Make changes	Enables everyone to make changes to the contents of the folder or volume (including adding new items or deleting existing items) when accessing your computer from another computer.

7. Select or deselect the Make all currently enclosed folders like this one check box.

   This option makes the access privileges of all folders inside the selected folder or disk exactly the same as the access privileges of its parent folder or disk.

   When you share a folder or disk for the first time, System 7 uses this option automatically. If you modify some of the settings and want the folders or disks to have consistent settings, you must select this option.

8. Select or deselect the Can't be moved, renamed, or deleted check box.

   Selecting this box prevents anyone (including the owner) from moving, renaming, or deleting this folder or disk.

9. Select or deselect the Same as enclosing folder check box. This box appears only for folders within shared folders.

   When you select this box, the folder assumes the access privilege assignments of its enclosing folder. If you move the selected folder into a new enclosing folder, its access privileges change to those of the new enclosing folder.

10. Close the Sharing window.

To change a folder's ownership

1. Connect your computer to a shared disk.

2. Select the folder for which you want to change the ownership (the folder must be one that you own).

3. From the File menu, select Sharing.

4. From the Owner pop-up menu, select the name of the user or group you want to assign ownership.

5. Close the Sharing window.

6. Click OK to save the changes.

Caution

Before you change ownership of your folder to another user, consider that the new owner can restrict or remove your access privileges entirely.

If, however, you change your folder's ownership to another user or group, then delete that user or group, the folder's ownership reverts to you.

Notes

The following are common ways to limit access.

To give all privilege to all users
When you first share a folder, this setting is the default.

If you change the settings, but later want to grant full access, select all three access options for Owner and Everyone. Because Everyone includes every user and group, you do not need to select any options for User/Group.

To keep a folder or disk completely private
Deselect all access options for User/Group and all access options for Everyone.

To share with only one user or group
From the pop-up menu, select the user or group with which you want to share access. Next, select all three access options for that user or group. Then, deselect all three access options for Everyone.

To keep a folder private, but enable others to drop items into the folder
Select the Make changes check box for Everyone, then deselect all other options for User/Group and Everyone.

See also *Privacy* and *Users & Groups Control Panel*.

Accessing Other Computers

Purpose

Enables you to use or to store information on another computer's hard drive. You can store information temporarily (if you need extra space) or permanently.

You access other computers on networks only.

To access another computer on the network

1. Open the Chooser.

   If the Chooser does not appear on the Apple menu, use the Finder's Find command to locate it.

2. Enable AppleTalk by clicking the Active button (if this button is not already selected).

   Even if you use EtherNet to connect to other computers on the network, you must enable AppleTalk.

3. Click the AppleShare icon.

4. If your network is divided into zones (if zone names appear in the lower left corner of the Chooser window), click the zone in which the computer you want to access resides.

   If your network is not divided into zones, skip this step.

5. Click the name of the computer you want to use.

6. Click OK.

   A password dialog box asks you to connect as a guest or as a registered user.

7. If you are not a registered user on that computer, click Guest.

   If you are a registered user, type your name and password (as that computer's owner identifies you).

8. Select the name of the shared disk(s) you want to use. You can type the first part of a disk's name to find it.

    To select more than one disk, hold down the **Shift** or **Command** (⌘) key as you select subsequent disks.

9. To access shared disks or folders at startup, click the check box(es) to the right of those disk(s) or folder(s).

    If you are a registered user, click the Save my name only or Save my name and password check box.

    If the computer saves your password, anyone can start your computer and access the other computer's files, so use this option with care.

10. Click OK.

11. Close the Chooser.

To access shared disks using an alias

1. Access another computer on the network (follow the preceding set of steps, but do not close the Chooser).

2. Click the shared disk's icon.

3. From the File menu, select Make Alias. For more information about aliases, see *Aliases*.

4. If you want to use a different name, rename the alias.

5. Drag the alias's icon to a convenient place on your disk.

6. The next time you want to access that shared disk, double-click its alias.

    If you originally accessed the computer as a guest user, you access the disk as a guest user and no password dialog box appears.

    If you originally accessed the computer as a registered user, the password dialog box appears. Type your password.

Note

See also *Privacy* and *Users & Groups Control Panel*.

Aliases

Purpose

Enables you to have a copy of an application or
document in more than one place without using disk
space to store the application or document multiple
times.

An alias is a copy of an icon; folders, disks, documents,
applications, and even the Trash can have aliases.

To create an alias

1. In the Finder, select the item for which you want to
   create an alias.

2. From the File menu, select Make Alias.

To delete an alias

Delete an alias in the same way you delete other files—
place it in the Trash.

To find the original document associated with an alias

1. Select the alias whose original document you want to
   find.

2. From the File menu, select Get Info.

   or

   Press ⌘-I.

   The Finder displays displays the Get Info window.

To create more than one alias

You can create an alias of an alias, but this method is not
the best way to create a second (or subsequent) alias. If
you delete the first alias, you also lose your second (and
any subsequent) alias because the second alias does not
point to the original file.

To create more than one alias, create each alias from the original file; then deleting the first alias has no effect.

To use an alias for remote access

1. Enable remote access on your computer. For instructions, see *Remote Access*.

2. Create an alias of your hard disk, and move it to a floppy disk.

3. When you need to access your computer from another computer on your network, load the floppy disk and double-click the alias of your hard disk.

   If possible, the network establishes a link to your computer.

Notes

By default, an alias has the same icon as its original file, whether that icon is a default or customized icon; however, an alias (like any other item) can have its own icon. For more information on custom icons, see *Icons*.

Names of aliases appear in italic type. When you create an alias, the name of the alias is the name of the original document plus the word *Alias*. For example, System 7 names an alias of the Puzzle desk accessory *Puzzle Alias*. Because you can rename an alias, the italic type—rather than the word *Alias*—is the most reliable indicator of an alias.

You can copy, rename, or move an alias without affecting access to the original file. You also can copy, rename, or move the original file.

If you create an alias of a document stored on removable media (such as a floppy disk) and System 7 cannot find the document, System 7 prompts you to insert the appropriate disk when you double-click the alias.

If you create an alias of a document stored on another computer, and that computer is not available to your system when you double-click the alias, your computer attempts to create a link to that computer in order to open the file. This procedure is a handy way to set up a network connection quickly.

See also *Apple Menu Items Folder*, *Icons*, *Remote Access*, and *Startup Items Folder*.

Apple Menu Items Folder

Purpose

Contains all items that appear in the Apple menu.

System 7 stores the Apple Menu Items folder in the System Folder.

To install an item in the Apple menu

To install an item in the Apple menu, drag the item into the Apple Menu Items folder. You can install desk accessories, documents, applications, aliases, or individual control panels in the Apple menu.

The Apple menu displays the first 50 items (according to alphabetical order) in the Apple Menu Items folder.

To remove an item from the Apple menu

To remove an item from the Apple menu, drag the item out of the Apple Menu Items folder (and out of the System Folder).

Note

See also *Aliases* and *System Folder*.

Application Menu

Purpose

Indicates which applications are running and which application is active. You also can use the Application menu to switch from one application to another and to show or hide an application's windows.

System 7 indicates the Application menu with an icon at the right end of the menu bar.

To make an open application active

1. To safeguard your work, save any work in progress before switching to another application.

2. From the Application menu, select the application you want to make active.

   or

   Click anywhere in the window of the application you want to make active.

   or

   From the Finder, select the icon of the application you want to make active.

   The application you select becomes the active application.

To hide the active application

From the Application menu, select the Hide command. (The complete name of the Hide command varies, depending on the current application. For example, if the current application is Excel, the command is Hide Excel.)

System 7 hides the windows of the active application and dims the application's name in the Application menu. When you hide the current application, another application (usually the Finder) becomes active.

To hide all applications except the active application

From the Application menu, select Hide Others.

System 7 hides all windows other than the windows of the active application and dims the names of those applications in the Application menu.

To show all open applications

From the Application menu, select Show All.

System 7 shows all the windows of all open applications. Some windows may be covered by other windows.

Caution

When an application other than the active application requires your attention, System 7 flashes that application's icon at the top of the Application menu. Switch to that application and determine what it needs.

For example, if the printer runs out of paper while you are printing in the background, Print Monitor flashes a printer icon at the top of the Application menu. Selecting Print Monitor from the Application menu enables Print Monitor to display a dialog box that tells you that the printer is out of paper.

Notes

The bottom section of the application menu lists all open applications in alphabetical order. The Finder is always open.

Hiding applications speeds up background processing because the computer uses less time to refresh the screen. If you do not hide applications, each application updates its portion of the screen every time you move an item.

Automatic Updating

Purpose

Automatically updates documents with information
from other documents (even in another application or on
another computer on the network) whenever you modify
the source documents.

Automatic updating is essentially a real time Copy and
Paste feature. This feature is especially useful for
managing documents that several people in a work
group prepare in separate parts. A classic example is
a budget report, where one person is responsible for
spreadsheets, another person for charts, another person
for text, and yet another person for combining the parts
into a whole.

Automatic updating is available in several applications
programs. To learn whether an application supports
automatic updating, check whether the application's Edit
menu includes Create Publisher and Subscribe To
commands. If the application does not include these
commands, contact the software publisher for upgrade
information.

Publishers

A *publisher* is the portion of a document that System 7
makes available to other documents or applications. You
can *publish* more than one part of a document. Published
documents can include text or graphics.

To create a publisher

1. Select the part of the active document that you want
   to include in another document.

2. From the Edit menu, select Create Publisher.

   System 7 creates a separate file, called an edition, that
   identifies that part of that document.

3. Name the edition.

4. Click OK.

To set publisher options

1. Select the publisher for which you want to set options.

2. From the Edit menu, select Publisher Options.

   System 7 displays a dialog box that contains the publisher options.

3. To see the edition's location, click the arrow of the pop-up menu at the top of the screen.

4. Set the Send Editions option.

   Select Save to update the edition whenever you save the publisher.

   Select Manually to update the edition only when you click the Send Edition Now button.

   The date and time in the bottom left corner of the dialog box indicate when you or System 7 last sent the edition.

5. To send the edition now, regardless of the Send Editions option setting, click the Send Edition Now button.

6. To cancel the publisher (and sever the link between the publishing document and the edition), click the Cancel Publisher button.

7. To put a border around the publishers or subscribers in the current document, select Show Borders (if available—not every application supports the Show Borders command).

8. To save the changes to your settings, click OK; otherwise, click Cancel.

To restore a cancelled publisher

Cancelling the publisher removes the link between the publisher and the specified edition file. This command does not delete the edition file, but the publisher can no longer update the edition. You cannot reverse this command; after you cancel the publisher and save the document, you cannot reestablish the link.

If you cancel the publisher inadvertently, you have two options:

- If you have not saved the document, select the Revert command from the File menu (if available) or close the document (cancelling any changes you made) and then open the document again.

- If you do not want to lose your other changes, or you already closed the document, select the area you want to publish (the same area as the preceding publisher), then create an edition with the same name and the same location as the preceding edition.

Editions

An *edition* is a copy of the published data that System 7 stores on your hard disk as a separate file. The publisher writes to the edition, and the subscriber reads from the edition.

To use unmounted editions

When a subscribing document is on an unmounted volume, the computer prompts you to insert the volume (if on removable media) or attempts to connect to the appropriate File Sharing or AppleShare volume.

To share editions only

To enable users to subscribe to various documents, but not to change the original publisher, store the publisher in a folder without access privileges and the editions in a folder with access privileges.

To use nested editions

You can create editions that contain other editions. After you set the appropriate options in the publisher and subscriber, System 7 updates the subscriber with changes to either original document.

For example, suppose that you create an edition of a chart from a business charting program and use that chart in a graphics program. In the graphics program, you create a snazzier border and some special graphics for the chart. Then, you create an edition of the modified chart.

The new edition is a *nested edition* because it contains an edition. From this point, you place the modified chart (the nested edition) in a page-layout program and add text that describes the chart.

When you update the chart in the business charting program, System 7 automatically updates the chart in the graphics and page-layout programs. When you update the chart in the graphics program, System 7 automatically updates the chart in the page-layout program.

To display information about an edition

1. From the Finder, double-click the edition for which you want to see information.

   System 7 displays the edition's contents, the edition's type (TEXT or PICT), and an Open Publisher button.

2. To open the publisher, click the Open Publisher button.

To use the edition

1. Place the cursor where you want to insert the edition.

2. From the Edit menu, select Subscribe To.

3. Click the icon of the edition to which you want to subscribe.

4. Click OK.

Subscribers

A *subscriber* is the section of a document that obtains its data from other documents or applications via an edition.

To reposition the subscriber

1. Select the subscriber you want to reposition.

2. From the Edit menu, select Cut.

   or

   Press ⌘-X.

3. Move the cursor to the location where you want to insert the subscriber.

4. From the Edit menu, select Paste.

   or

   Press ⌘-V.

To set subscriber options

1. Select the subscriber for which you want to set options.

2. From the Edit menu, select Subscriber Options.

   System 7 displays a dialog box that contains the subscriber options.

3. To see the edition's location, click the arrow of the pop-up menu at the top of the screen.

4. Set the Get Editions option.

   Select Automatically to update the subscriber whenever the publisher updates the edition.

   Select Manually to update the subscriber only when you click the Get Edition Now button.

The date and time in the bottom left corner of the
window indicate when you or System 7 last sent the
edition.

5. To get the edition now, regardless of the Get Editions
   setting, click the Get Edition Now button.

6. To cancel the subscriber (and sever the link between
   the subscribing document and the edition), click the
   Cancel Subscriber button.

7. To open the publisher for editing, click the Open
   Publisher button.

8. To put a border around the publishers or subscribers
   in the current document, select Show Borders
   (if available—not every application supports the
   Show Borders command).

9. To save the changes to your settings, click OK;
   otherwise, click Cancel.

To edit subscribers

Because System 7 updates subscribers periodically, do
not waste your time making changes that you will lose
with the next subscriber update.

For text subscribers, you cannot edit the text, but you
can set the font, size, or style of the entire subscriber.

For graphic subscribers, you can reposition the
subscriber, but (in most cases) you cannot resize it.
In cases where you can resize the graphic subscriber,
resizing handles appear on the corners of the subscriber.
You cannot change the text in a graphic subscriber; you
can change the text only in the publisher.

In all cases, when you change items in the publisher,
those changes appear in all subscribers to that publisher.

Notes

System 7 does not save an edition unless you save its
publisher.

When you delete a publisher, any related editions remain on the Desktop. You cannot modify or change these editions, but you can use them in new subscribers.

See also *System Folder*.

CDEVs (Control Panel Devices)

System 7 stores CDEVs, or Control Panel Devices, in the Control Panels folder within the System Folder, rather than in the System Folder itself.

See also *Control Panels Folder*.

Clean Up

Aligns all icons in a Finder window to the nearest position on the Finder's invisible grid.

With System 7, you can make Clean Up automatic and you can select whether the Finder displays icons in straight or staggered rows (via the Views Control Panel).

To clean up a Finder window

1. From the View menu, select By Icon or By Small Icon.

2. To move all icons into rows (staggered or not staggered, as specified in the Views Control Panel), select Clean Up Window from the Special menu.

To clean up by name or size (special)

1. From the View menu, select the way you want to arrange (view) your icons: By Name, By Size, and so on.

2. From the View menu, select By Icon or By Small Icon.

3. Hold down the **Option** key as you select Clean Up Special from the Special menu.

To clean up the Desktop

To move all items on the Desktop to their nearest grid position, select Clean Up Desktop from the Special menu.

To clean up all

To move all items on the Desktop into rows at the right of the screen, hold down the **Option** key as you select Clean Up All from the Special menu.

To clean up selected items

1. Select the item(s) you want to align.

2. Hold down the **Shift** key as you select Clean Up Selection from the Special menu.

Note

See also *Views Control Panel*.

Communications Toolbox

Enables applications to communicate with other computers. The user does not access the Communications Toolbox directly.

The communications tools enable the applications to do the following:

- Exchange data with other applications (on the same or other computers).

- Enable the user to browse through a listing of applications that can exchange data.

- Verify user identities across a network.

Previous System versions stored communications tools in a Communications folder (in the System Folder). System 7 stores communications tools in the Extensions folder (in the System Folder).

See also *Extensions Folder* and *System Folder*.

Control Panels Folder

Contains control panels that enable you to set the following Macintosh controls.

Control Panel	Effect
Color	Enables you to adjust the highlight color and the window border colors.
Easy Access	Enables you to set mouse keys, sticky keys, and slow keys.
File Sharing Monitor	Enables you to monitor the level of File Sharing activity at your computer (the part of your Macintosh's time used by persons other than you).
General Controls	Enables you to adjust basic settings, such as the Desktop pattern, how fast the insertion bar cursor blinks; and how many times menu items blink when

Control Panel	*Effect*
	selected. Also enables you to set your Macintosh's date and time, including whether to display 12- or 24-hour time.
Keyboard	Enables you to set the keyboard repeat rate, which determines how long you have to hold down a key before the key starts repeating. If you installed more than one keyboard layout, also enables you to select the layout you want to use.
Labels	Enables you to edit the colors and text of items on the Finder's Label menu.
Map	Displays a world map and enables you to determine distances between cities. Also enables you to change your Macintosh's clock by making a different city current.
Memory	Enables you to control the disk cache, virtual memory, and 32-bit addressing options.
Monitors	Enables you to set, position (relative to one another), and specify the number of colors on each of your monitors.
Mouse	Enables you to set the mouse speed and the double-click speed.
Sharing Setup	Enables you to set up the File Sharing feature.

Control Panel	Effect
Sound	Enables you to specify the sound your Macintosh uses as its "beep." For Macintoshes with sound input capability, also enables you to record and use new sounds as the "beep."
Startup Disk	Enables you to select the hard disk you want to use as the startup volume.
Users & Groups	Enables you to define users and groups for File Sharing.
Views	Enables you to customize icon and list views in Finder windows.

System 7 stores control panels in the Control Panels folder within the System Folder, rather than in the System Folder itself.

Note

See also *Easy Access Control Panel*, *File Sharing Monitor Control Panel*, *Labels Control Panel*, *Memory Control Panel*, *Sharing Setup Control Panel*, *System Folder*, *Users & Groups Control Panel*, and *Views Control Panel*.

Data Access Language

Data Access Language (DAL) enables you to connect your Macintosh to mainframe computers.

System 7 stores DAL files in the Preferences folder (in the System Folder).

To get information from a remote system

1. From the File menu, select the Open Query command.

2. Select the query you want to use.

   The application connects to the remote computer and retrieves the information.

3. Manipulate the data on the Macintosh, integrating it into other documents.

Notes

Computers send query documents in only one language, Data Access Language, regardless of the host computer, database, or network.

To translate the DAL commands to a form the host computer understands, the host computer must have a DAL server program installed. Your Macintosh must have the DAL system extension in the Extensions folder (in the System Folder).

See also *System Folder*.

Desk Accessories

Purpose

Desk accessories are small applications with limited functions.

Previous System versions stored desk accessories in suitcases, installed them in the System file, and placed them on the Apple menu. With System 7, you treat desk accessories like any other application.

To convert a desk accessory from a previous System version

1. Double-click the desk accessory's suitcase to open it.

   A window displays the contents of the suitcase.

2. Drag the desk accessories out of the window and place them wherever you want them (except the Trash).

   To make a desk accessory appear in the Apple menu, place the desk accessory or its alias in the Apple Menu Items folder (within the System Folder).

To use desk accessories with both System 6 and System 7

If you intend to use both System 6 and System 7, keep copies of your desk accessories in their old suitcases. The System 7 version of desk accessories cannot operate under previous System versions.

Caution

You cannot use System 7 desk accessories with previous System versions, and you cannot convert desk accessories back to previous System desk accessories. Be sure to keep a copy of desk accessories in their old suitcases.

Notes

After you liberate your desk accessories from the confines of their suitcases, the desk accessories become System 7 compatible applications. In System 7, little real difference exists between a desk accessory and an application: you can place either in the Apple menu, launch either by double-clicking, and install as many of either as you like (previous Systems limited the number of desk accessories you could install).

See also *Apple Menu Items Folder*.

Easy Access Control Panel

Purpose

Enables you to adjust the speed of mouse keys, slow keys, and sticky keys. This feature enables users who have difficulty using the mouse or keyboard to use their computer more easily.

To enable audio feedback

1. Open the Easy Access Control Panel (in the Control Panels folder within the System Folder).

2. To make the Macintosh whistle when you enable or disable features in the Easy Access Control Panel, select the Use on/off audio feedback check box.

   When you enable an item, the whistle slides up in pitch.

   When you disable an item, the whistle slides down in pitch.

3. Close the Easy Access Control Panel.

To disable audio feedback

1. Open the Easy Access Control Panel (in the Control Panels folder within the System Folder).

2. Deselect the Use on/off audio feedback check box.

3. Close the Easy Access Control Panel.

To enable mouse keys

The mouse keys feature enables you to use the numeric keypad on your keyboard to move the cursor (rather than or in addition to the mouse).

1. Open the Easy Access Control Panel (in the Control Panels folder within the System Folder).

2. In the Mouse Keys section of the Easy Access Control Panel, click the On button.

3. To set a delay for the mouse action, adjust the Initial Delay setting by clicking the appropriate button from the series of five buttons.

4. To set the speed at which the mouse moves, adjust the Maximum Speed setting by clicking the appropriate button from the series of eight buttons.

5. Close the Easy Access Control Panel.

To disable mouse keys

1. Open the Easy Access Control Panel (in the Control Panels folder within the System Folder).

2. In the Mouse Keys section of the Easy Access Control Panel, click the Off button.

3. Close the Easy Access Control Panel.

To enable slow keys

The slow keys feature prevents accidental keystrokes by increasing the time you must hold down a key in order for System 7 to recognize your keystroke.

You can use slow keys and sticky keys at the same time. (The sticky keys feature is described later in this section.)

1. Open the Easy Access Control Panel (in the Control Panels folder within the System Folder).

2. In the Slow Keys section of the Easy Access Control Panel, click the On button.

3. Adjust the Acceptance Delay.

4. To hear a "key click" when System 7 accepts a keystroke, select the Use key click sound check box.

5. Close the Easy Access Control Panel.

To disable slow keys

1. Open the Easy Access Control Panel (in the Control Panels folder within the System Folder).

2. In the Slow Keys section of the Easy Access Control
   Panel, click the Off button.

3. Close the Easy Access Control Panel.

To enable sticky keys

The sticky keys feature enables you to type keystroke
combinations without actually pressing the keys at the
same time. A keystroke combination normally requires
that you hold down a modifier key (Shift, Option,
Command, or Control) as you press the other key.

You can use slow keys and sticky keys at the same time.

1. Open the Easy Access Control Panel (in the Control
   Panels folder within the System Folder).

2. In the Sticky Keys section of the Easy Access Control
   Panel, click the On button.

3. To hear a "beep" when System 7 sets a modifier
   keystroke, select the Beep when modifier key is set
   check box.

4. Close the Easy Access Control Panel.

To disable sticky keys

1. Open the Easy Access Control Panel (in the Control
   Panels folder within the System Folder).

2. In the Sticky Keys section of the Easy Access Control
   Panel, click the Off button.

3. Close the Easy Access Control Panel.

Note

See also *Control Panels Folder* and *System Folder*.

Extensions Folder

Contains extensions to the system, such as ImageWriter and LaserWriter drivers, network information, and communications tools.

System 7 stores the Extensions folder in the System Folder.

To review which printers are installed

1. Open the Extensions folder (in the System Folder).

2. Review which printers are installed (printer drivers are Chooser documents).

   If printers you never use are installed, you can delete them.

3. After reviewing the contents of the folder, close the Extensions folder's window.

To avoid startup document compatibility problems

1. If your Macintosh crashes before startup is complete, restart the computer while holding down the Shift key.

   Your Macintosh displays

   ```
   Welcome to Macintosh
   ```

   and

   ```
   Extensions off
   ```

   This step should avoid any incompatibility problems.

2. Follow the next set of steps to determine which items in the Extensions folder are causing problems.

To find a problem extension

1. Remove an item from the Extensions folder. Do not remove any item that came with System 7.

2. Restart the computer without holding down the Shift key.

    If the computer no longer crashes, that extension was creating the problem.

    Keep that extension out of the System Folder and the Extensions folder, and contact the extension's developer for an upgrade.

    If the computer still crashes, return that extension to the Extensions folder.

3. Repeat steps 1 and 2, removing other items, until you locate the source of the problem.

Note

See also *System Folder*.

File Sharing

Purpose

Enables you to share files, folders, and volumes (disks) with other users on a network. The other users can use shared disks and folders on your computer, and you can use shared disks and folders on their computers.

File Sharing is built-in software, unlike network add-ons such as TOPS or AppleShare. File Sharing is a feature new to System 7.

To enable File Sharing

1. Connect the Macintoshes on the network with Apple's LocalTalk, Farallon's PhoneNet, or equivalent cables.

2. Use the Sharing Setup Control Panel to start File Sharing. For more information, see *Sharing Setup Control Panel*.

3. Use the Users & Groups Control Panel to configure users and groups. Make any necessary changes to the Guest user's status. For more information, see *Users & Groups Control Panel.*

4. Select the folders or volumes you want to share.

5. From the File menu, select Sharing.

6. Select the options you want to use. For more information about these options, see *Access Privileges.*

To use files shared by others

To access files, folders, and volumes shared by others, use the Chooser. For more information, see *Accessing Other Computers.*

To stop File Sharing for all users

1. Open the Sharing Setup Control Panel (in the Control Panels folder within the System Folder).

2. Click the Stop button in the File Sharing section of the Sharing Setup Control Panel.

   System 7 displays the following message:

   ```
   How many minutes until File Sharing
   is disabled?
   ```

3. Type the number of minutes before File Sharing stops. Provide enough time for users to save any work in progress.

4. Click OK to stop File Sharing or click Cancel to keep File Sharing in effect.

   If you click OK, System 7 disconnects all users at the time you specified.

5. Close the Sharing Setup Control Panel.

To stop File Sharing for specified users

1. Open the File Sharing Monitor Control Panel (in the Control Panels folder within the System Folder).

2. Select the user or users you want to disconnect. (Shift-click to select the second and subsequent users.)

3. Click the Disconnect button.

   System 7 displays the following message:

   ```
   How many minutes until user is
   disconnected?
   ```

4. Type the number of minutes before System 7 disconnects these users. Provide enough time for users to save any work in progress.

5. Click OK.

6. Close the File Sharing Monitor Control Panel.

To disable File Sharing for a specific folder or volume

1. Select the folder or volume for which you want to disable File Sharing.

2. From the File menu, select Sharing.

3. Deselect the Share this item and its contents check box.

To use File Sharing with previous System versions

On a network, the files, folders, and volumes shared by Macintoshes that use System 7 are also available to Macintoshes that use a previous System version; however, the Macintoshes that use a previous System version cannot make their own files, folders, and volumes available to other computers on the network.

Macintoshes that use a previous System version must have the AppleShare INIT installed in their System Folders. The AppleShare INIT is the System extension that enables all users (whether or not their computers use

System 7) to connect to AppleShare or File Sharing volumes. You can use the Installer to install this option.

To choose between File Sharing and AppleShare

AppleShare requires a dedicated Macintosh (a *server*), which is too expensive for many small companies.

File Sharing, which is included with System 7, provides a limited version of AppleShare. File Sharing eliminates the "SneakerNet" approach to sharing information (carrying disks from one computer to another on floppy disks), but has the following limitations:

- File Sharing uses at least 250K of RAM on each Macintosh; however, because RAM is less expensive than a dedicated Macintosh with a hard disk (even when you purchase RAM for several machines), File Sharing can be more cost-effective than AppleShare.

- File Sharing diverts processing capability from other work, degrading performance noticeably.

- File Sharing can serve only 10 folders or volumes from one Macintosh at one time, and can support only 50 users. In practice, the System bogs down long before you reach these theoretical limits.

- Macintoshes sharing files must remain on to ensure that the files are available to other users.

You also can use File Sharing in conjunction with AppleShare, choosing the appropriate method of sharing for each situation:

- To send a few documents to another user on the network, use File Sharing to share the appropriate folder or folders.

  With File Sharing, the other user copies the information directly. If you used AppleShare, you would have to copy the documents to the AppleShare server, and the other user would have to copy the documents from there.

• To share a database among a number of users, use AppleShare rather than burdening one user's computer with all the network traffic.

Note

See also *Access Privileges*, *Sharing*, *Sharing Setup Control Panel*, and *Users & Groups Control Panel*.

File Sharing Monitor Control Panel

Purpose

Enables you to verify who is using your computer, how much network activity is occurring on your computer, and what folders and disks you are currently sharing.

To check the level of File Sharing activity on your computer

1. Open the File Sharing Monitor Control Panel (in the Control Panels folder within the System Folder).

2. Review the File Sharing Activity thermometer.

   If the thermometer is close to the busy side (rather than the idle side), your computer is spending most of its processing time on File Sharing.

   The activity level changes continuously, so the average level, not a momentary peak, is the true measure of activity.

3. Close the File Sharing Monitor Control Panel.

To see which folders and disks you are sharing

1. Open the File Sharing Monitor Control Panel (in the Control Panels folder within the System Folder).

2. Review the list of folders and disks under the heading Shared Items.

3. Close the File Sharing Monitor Control Panel.

To see which users are currently connected

1. Open the File Sharing Monitor Control Panel (in the Control Panels folder within the System Folder).

2. Review the list of users under the heading Connected Users.

3. Close the File Sharing Monitor Control Panel.

To disconnect specified users

1. Open the File Sharing Monitor Control Panel (in the Control Panels folder within the System Folder).

2. Select the user or users you want to disconnect. (Shift-click to select the second and subsequent users.)

3. Click the Disconnect button.

   System 7 displays the following message:

   How many minutes until user is disconnected?

4. Type the number of minutes before System 7 disconnects these users. Provide enough time for the users to save any work in progress.

5. Click OK.

6. Close the File Sharing Monitor Control Panel.

Notes

If your computer is consistently busy with File Sharing, it is less available to you, so you may want to restrict usage by relocating the most heavily used files to a more convenient computer or by limiting the number of users who have access to your computer.

If the network is consistently busy with File Sharing, dedicating a computer to File Sharing using AppleShare may be more cost-effective.

See also *Access Privileges*, *File Sharing*, *Network Extension File*, and *Users & Groups Control Panel*.

File Sharing Extension File

For File Sharing to operate properly, the File Sharing extension file and the Network Extension file must be located in the Extensions folder (in the System Folder) and the Sharing Setup Control Panel and the Users & Groups Control Panel must be located in the Control Panels folder (in the System Folder).

See also *Control Panels Folder*, *Extensions Folder*, *Network Extension File*, *System Folder*, and *Users & Groups Control Panel*.

Find Command

Purpose

Enables the user to find the locations of files. You can search by name, size, kind, label, date created, date modified, version, comments, and whether the file is locked.

Previous System versions included a desk accessory named Find File. System 7 includes a Find command on the File menu. The differences between Find and Find File include the following:

- Find is more flexible than Find File, enabling you to search by a variety of criteria, rather than just by the file name.

- Find displays the locations of the files and opens folders if necessary. Find File simply displayed the path name.

- Find is available only in the Finder, but in System 7 the Finder is always open.

To find documents, applications, and folders by name

1. From the File menu, select Find.

   or

   Press ⌘-F.

2. In the Find text box, type the name (or any part of the name) of the item you want to find.

3. Click the Find button.

   Find searches all available disks to locate the first item that meets the specified criteria.

   Find opens the window for the folder or volume where the item is located and highlights the item.

4. To find the next item that meets the same criteria, select Find Again from the File menu.

   or

   Press ⌘-G.

To find documents, applications, and folders by other criteria

1 From the File menu, select Find.

   or

   Press ⌘-F.

2. If the More Choices button appears in the lower left corner, click it; otherwise, skip this step.

3. From the left pop-up menu, select the search criterion.

4. From the center pop-up menu, select the search option.

5. In the text box at the right, type the value for which you want to search.

   If you are searching by date, click the part of the date you want to change (day, month, or year), then click the arrows to the right of the date to adjust that part of the date.

6. From the Search pop-up menu, select the volume you want to search. If any window is active, the volume for that window is already selected.

   or

   From the Search pop-up menu, select Selected items (to search only the items selected on the Desktop).

7. To display all the items at one time, select the All at once check box. If you are searching all disks, this option is dimmed.

   To display the items sequentially, deselect the All at once check box.

8. Click Find.

To return to searching by name

1. From the File menu, select Find.

   or

   Press ⌘-F.

2. Click the Fewer Choices button.

To perform a multiple-stage search

1. From the File menu, select Find.

   or

   Press ⌘-F.

2. If the More Choices button appears in the lower left corner, click it; otherwise, skip this step.

3. From the left pop-up menu, select the search criteria.

4. From the center pop-up menu, select the search method.

5. In the text box at the right, type the value for which you want to search.

   If you are searching by date, click the part of the date you want to change (day, month, or year), then click the arrows to the right of the date to adjust that part of the date.

6. From the Search pop-up menu, select the volume you want to search. If any window is active, the volume for that window is already selected.

7. Select the All at once check box.

8. Click Find.

9. From the File menu, select Find.

   or

   Press ⌘-F.

10. If the More Choices button appears in the lower left corner, click it; otherwise, skip this step.

11. From the left pop-up menu, select the search criteria for the next stage of the search.

12. From the center pop-up menu, select the search method for the next stage of the search.

13. In the text box at the right, type the value for which you want to search.

    If you are searching by date, click the part of the date you want to change (day, month, or year), then click the arrows to the right of the date to adjust that part of the date.

14. From the Search pop-up menu, select Selected items (rather than a volume name).

15. Select the All at once check box.

16. Click Find.

    System 7 displays all the items that meet both search criteria.

You can perform additional searches by repeating steps 9-16.

To use Find for quick backups

To make a quick backup, you can use the Find command to locate all files modified after a certain date, and then copy those files to removable media.

1. From the File menu, select Find.

   or

   Press ⌘-F.

2. If the More Choices button appears in the lower left corner, click it; otherwise, skip this step.

3. From the left pop-up menu, select Date Modified.

4. From the center pop-up menu, select is after.

5. Click the part of the date you want to change (day, month, or year), then click the arros to the right of the date to adjust that part of the date.

6. From the Search pop-up menu, select the volume you want to search. If any window is active, the volume for that window is already selected.

7. Select the All at once check box.

8. Click Find.

9. Drag the highlighted file icons to the icon of the disk where you want to back up the files.

Search criteria

Criterion	Description
Name	Specify the name (or any part of the name) of the item in the selection box and search for any file name that contains, starts with, ends with, or does not contain that text.

Criterion	*Description*
Size	Specify a file size (in kilobytes) and search for items greater than or less than that size. This feature is especially handy if you need to make more space on your hard disk and want to see what large items you can remove.
Kind	Select from Folder, Alias, Chooser Extension, Desk Accessory, System Extension, Application program, and documents (listed according to their creator document). You can search for all documents created by a specific application.
Label	Specify a label and search for files that are or are not associated with the label, or files that are or are not associated with any label.
Date Created	Specify a date and search for files created on, before, after, or not on that date.
Date Modified	Specify a date and search for files last modified on, before, after, or not on that date. You can use this option in conjunction with the All at once check box to make a quick bckup.
Version	Specify a version number (for applications only) and search for items that match, are befre, are after, or are not equal to the secified version number.

Criterion	Description
Comments	Enter text and search for items that do or do not contain that text. Be aware, however, that comments disappear whenever you rebuild the Desktop file (such as when you install System 7).
Lock	Specify whether to search for items that are or are not locked.

Notes

The Find command cannot locate items within the System file (such as installed fonts and sounds). To find items within the System file, double-click the System file icon, then browse through the System file's window.

See also *System Folder*.

Finder

Purpose

The Finder has many new features in System 7. Some changes are fundamental, such as the new method of hndling desk accessories. Some changes are cosmetic, such as the new window border coloring and 3-D window effects.

This entry presents the features of the Finder that are new to System 7 and not covered in another section. The features covered in other sections are referenced in the Notes.

To learn about your Macintosh

From the Apple menu, select About this Macintosh.

System 7 displays the amount of available memory and indicates how the computer is using the rest of the memory.

To see the original Finder screen, hold down the Option key while selecting the About this Macintosh command.

To use automatic crolling

If you drag icons (in icon views) or item names (in list views) to the boundary of a window, the window scrolls in that direction when the cursor reaches the window boundary.

To change the display order of list views

To change the heading by which System 7 sorts items in list views, click the heading (Name, Size, Kind, and so on) you want to use for sorting.

The order of the list changes immediately.

You also can use the View menu to change the sort heading.

To change window border colors

1. Opethe Color Control Panel (in the Control Panels folder within the System Folder).

2. Select a color from the pop-up menu: Standard (Purple), Gold, Green, Turquoise, Red, Pink, Blue, Gray, or Black &White.

3. Close the Color Control Panel.

To open a window's parent folder

1. Hold down the Command (⌘) key and click the window's title.

   System 7 displays a pop-up menu that shows the folder hierarchy.

2. Hold down the Option key and move the mouse down one level in the menu.

3. Release the mouse button.

   To close the window while opening the parent folder, release the mouse button and the **Option** key.

To copy files in the background

1. Open the application you want to use while the Finder is copying.

2. Select the files you want to copy.

3. If the destination for the copied files is on another disk, drag the files to their destination.

   If the destination for the copied files is on the same disk, hold down the **Option** key as you drag the files to their destination.

   The Finder starts to copy the files.

4. Click the window of the application you want to use.

To select items in Finder windows

When you use a selection rectangle to select icons (in icon views) or item names (in list views), System 7 highlights an icon whenever the selection rectangle touches any part of the icon.

Previous System versions highlighted only those icons completely enclosed by the selection rectangle, and only after you released the mouse. In addition, previous System versions did not enable you to use a selection rectangle in list views.

To select items by using the keyboard

Selecting items by using the keyboard is a great deal easier than with earlier Systems. The following keyboard shortcuts work in Finder windows, in the Chooser, and in directory dialog boxes.

- You can select items by typing the first letter(s) of the file name. System 7 selects the first item that begins with the letter(s) you type.

  If no item begins with those letters, System 7 selects the next item (alphabetically).

  If no item begins with letters that are after the letters you typed, System 7 selects the last item in the list.

- You can move from one icon to another (in icon views) by using the arrow keys. System 7 selects the first icon in the direction of the arrow key you press.

- The Tab key selects the next item alphabetically, except in directory dialog boxes, where Tab selects the next field.

- In Finder windows only, pressing Enter selects or deselects the item's name for editing.

To open a document with an application other than its creator

1. Select the document (or an alias of the document) you want to open.

2. Drag the document's icon onto the application's icon (or onto its alias). Do not release the mouse button.

   If the application can open the document, System 7 highlights the application's icon.

   If the application cannot open the document, return the document to its former position.

3. Release the mouse button.

   The document's icon returns to its original location, and the application opens a copy of the document.

To use outline views of folders

When you display folders in list view (rather than in icon view), you now can list folders in outline form. This feature enables you to display not only the contents of those folders, but also the contents of the folders they contain.

In list views, a triangle appears to the left of each folder name. When the folder's contents are hidden, the triangle points toward the folder's name. When the folder's contents are displayed, the triangle points down and the names of the items in that folder are indented below the folder's name.

To show a folder's contents in outline view, click the triangle to the left of the folder. To show additional levels of folders, click the appropriate triangles.

To hide a folder's contents, click its triangle a second time.

To select or copy items from different folders in one step, you can click the first item and then Shift-click the additional items, or you can drag the selection rectangle to enclose all the items.

To rename an icon

1. Select the icon you want to rename.

   You cannot change the name of a locked item. To unlock an item, see *Get Info*.

2. Press **Enter**.

   System 7 selects the item's name for editing.

3. Type the new name for the icon.

   or

   Use the Cut (⌘-**X**), Copy (⌘-**C**), and Paste (⌘-**V**) commands to edit the name.

   You can use the Undo command only while the item's name is selected.

4. Press **Enter** again.

   System 7 deselects the item's name.

To change only part of an icon's name

1. Select the icon you want to rename.

   You cannot change the name of a locked item. To unlock an item, see *Get Info*.

2. Press **Enter**.

   System 7 selects the item's name for editing.

3. Click and drag the mouse to select the part of the name you want to change.

4. Type the new part of the name for the icon.

   or

   Use the Cut (⌘-X), Copy (⌘-C), and Paste (⌘-V) commands to edit the name.

   You can use the Undo command only while the item's name is selected.

5. Press **Enter** again.

   System 7 deselects the item's name.

To use smart copy and replace

When copying an item to a disk or folder that already contains an item by the same name, System 7 asks whether you want to replace the existing item. System 7 tells you which item is newer so you don't make any mistakes.

To use smart copy to copy a floppy disk to a hard disk

One of the "no-nos" of previous System versions was to drag a floppy disk's icon onto a hard disk's icon, attempting to replace the entire contents of the hard disk with that of the floppy.

In System 7, however, this action merely creates (on the hard disk) a folder that has the floppy disk's name and contains all the files from the floppy. You can use this technique to copy a floppy disk into a folder.

To use smart dragging

In previous System versions, when you dragged an item from one overlapping window to another, the Finder activated the source window as soon as you clicked an item in that window. Often, this change obscured the destination window.

In System 7, when you drag an item from one overlapping window to another, the Finder keeps the destination folder in the front. (This feature works only if you drag a single item.)

To use smart zoom boxes

To make the window only as large as it needs to be to enclose all the items, click the zoom box. System 7's Finder has smart zoom boxes, which can make the window smaller as well as larger.

To sort list view windows

To sort by a category in list views, click the name of that category. For example, click Name to sort by name or Kind to sort by kind.

Duplicate file names

In previous System versions, a duplicate of the file named Fred was named Copy of Fred. A duplicate of that file was named Copy of copy of Fred, and so on.

With System 7, the Finder names these two copies Fred copy and Fred copy 2.

Improved use of color

On color and grayscale Macintoshes that display at least 16 colors or shades of gray, "grayed" (dimmed) menu items are really gray. Previous System versions simulated gray by alternating black and white dots, making "grayed" text hard to read.

The Trash and other Finder icons now have a 3-D effect as a result of gray shadowing. Active windows have 3-D zoom boxes, scroll arrows, size boxes, and scroll bars. Inactive windows have gray borders rather than black. The entire Macintosh screen has a softer look.

In addition, you now can color window borders via the Color Control Panel.

Note

See also *Aliases*, *Apple Menu Items Folder*, *Application Menu*, *Clean Up*, *Find Command*, *Get Info*, *Help Menu*, *Labels Control Panel*, *Put Away*, *Screen Snapshots*, *Startup Items Folder*, *Stationery Pads*, *Trash*, and *Views Control Panel*.

Fonts

Purpose

Enables the System to display text and enables you to display text in a variety of forms.

To install a font

1. Drag the icon of the font you want to install onto the System Folder icon.

   The Finder asks whether to place the font in the System file.

2. Click OK.

   or

   Drag the icon of the font you want to install onto the System file's icon.

To remove a font

1. Double-click the System file's icon (in the System Folder).

   System 7 displays a window that contains the items in the System file.

2. Drag the font you want to remove out of the System file's window and out of the System Folder.

   The font is no longer available for use.

3. Place the font in any convenient location outside the System Folder.

To convert old font suitcases

Previous System versions stored fonts in suitcases
for use with the Font/DA Mover or Fifth Generation
System's Suitcase. System 7 stores fonts in the System
file without suitcases.

1. To convert these fonts, double-click the icon of the
   suitcase.

   System 7 displays a window that contains the items in
   the suitcase.

2. Drag the fonts from the suitcase window onto the
   System file's icon. System 7 installs the fonts in the
   System file.

   or

   If you do not want to install the fonts immediately,
   drag the fonts from the suitcase window into a
   Fonts folder that you created.

Notes

Fonts are no longer installed with the Font/DA Mover,
but are part of the System file. For PostScript fonts, you
should store the printer fonts (and AFM fonts, if any) in
the Extensions folder (in the System Folder) and install
the screen fonts in the System file (in the System
Folder).

See also *System Folder* and *TrueType Fonts*.

Get Info

Purpose

Enables you to enter and review information about
items.

To find the original document associated with an alias

1. Select the alias for which you want to find the original document.

2. From the File menu, select Get Info.

   or

   Press ⌘-**I**.

   The Finder displays the Get Info window. The complete path name appears after the word `Original`.

3. Close the Get Info window.

To lock an item

1. Select the icon of the item you want to lock.

2. From the File menu, select Get Info.

   or

   Press ⌘-**I**.

   The Finder displays the Get Info window.

3. Select the Locked check box.

4. Close the Get Info window.

To unlock an item

1. Select the icon of the item you want to unlock.

2. From the File menu, select Get Info.

   or

   Press ⌘-**I**.

   The Finder displays the Get Info window.

3. Deselect the Locked check box.

4. Close the Get Info window.

To change a document into a Stationery Pad

1. Select the icon of the document you want to change into a Stationery Pad.

2. From the File menu, select Get Info.

   or

   Press ⌘-**I**.

   The Finder displays the Get Info window.

3. Select the Stationery Pad check box in the lower right corner of the window.

   The document's icon changes to the Stationery Pad icon. For more information, see *Stationery Pads*.

4. Close the Get Info window.

To determine a Stationery Pad's creator

1. Select the Stationery Pad's icon.

2. From the File menu, select Get Info.

   or

   Press ⌘-**I**.

   The Finder displays the Get Info window. The Stationery Pad's creator appears after the word Kind.

3. Close the Get Info window.

To determine the size of a folder with Get Info

1. Select the folder for which you want to know the size.

2. From the File menu, select Get Info.

   or

   Press ⌘-**I**.

   The Finder displays the Get Info window. The folder's size appears after the word Size.

3. Close the Get Info window.

To change the amount of memory an application reserves

1. Select the icon of the program whose memory usage you want to change.

   You can change the amount of memory an application uses only when the program is on an unlocked disk or volume.

2. From the File menu, select Get Info.

   or

   Press ⌘-I.

   The Finder displays the Get Info window. In the lower right corner of the window, Get Info displays two values:

   Suggested size is the minimum amount of RAM to reserve for the program, as specified by the developer.

   Current size is the amount of RAM the program reserves for itself when you use it. (If you are working with a very large document, you may need to increase the Current size.)

3. Enter a new value for Current size.

   Type a number that is at least as large as the Suggested size; otherwise, the program may run very slowly or not at all. If you enter a number that is too large, however, you may not be able to run other applications at the same time.

4. Close the Get Info window.

Notes

You can determine the size of a folder with Get Info if you do not want to take the time to calculate folder sizes.

All Stationery Pads have the same icon, but you can use Get Info to learn which application created the Stationery Pad before you launch that application.

See also *Aliases, Icons, Stationery Pads*, and *Views Control Panel*.

Help Menu

Purpose

Displays information about an item when you point to the item with the mouse pointer. The information appears on-screen in a *help balloon*.

Most applications do not yet support Balloon Help.

To locate the Help menu

The Help menu appears near the right end of the menu bar, to the left of the Application menu. The Help menu's icon is a word balloon with a question mark inside.

To enable Balloon Help

1. From the Help menu, select Show Balloons.

2. Place the mouse pointer on any item on-screen.

   To trigger help, the mouse must remain in the same position for approximately one second.

   System 7 displays a description of the item in a balloon.

To get more information about Balloon Help

From the Help menu, select About Balloon Help.

To disable Balloon Help

From the Help menu, select Hide Balloons.

To show Finder shortcuts

From the Help menu, select Finder Shortcuts.

Notes

Although help balloons cover part of the screen, you can perform actions on items underneath the balloons.

See also *Application Menu.*

IAC

IAC is an abbreviation for InterApplication Communications, which enables two or more programs (on the same or different computers) to exchange information. IAC also is called Program Linking.

Because most currently available applications cannot take advantage of this feature, Program Linking will be of limited use to the average user for some time.

See also *Program Linking.*

Icons

Enables you to change any icon to a custom icon.

To copy an existing icon

1. Select the item whose icon you want to copy.
2. From the File menu, select Get Info.

    or

    Press ⌘-I.
3. Click the icon in the upper left corner of the Get Info window.

4. From the Edit menu, select Copy.

   or

   Press ⌘-C.

   System 7 copies the icon to the Clipboard.

5. Close the Get Info window.

6. Use the copied icon to replace an existing icon (see the following set of steps).

   or

   Paste the copied icon into the Scrapbook to store it.

   or

   Paste the icon into a graphics program for editing.

To replace an existing icon

1. Copy the new icon from a graphics program or the Scrapbook.

   The picture you use for an icon can be any size, but the picture shrinks to fit if it is larger than 32-by-32 pixels.

2. Select the item whose icon you want to replace.

3. From the File menu, select Get Info.

   or

   Press ⌘-I.

4. Click the icon in the upper left corner of the Get Info window.

5. From the Edit menu, select Paste.

   or

   Press ⌘-V.

   System 7 replaces the icon.

6. Close the Get Info window.

To return an item's icon to the default icon

1. Select the item whose icon you want to return to the default icon.

2. From the File menu, select Get Info.

   or

   Press ⌘-I.

3. Click the icon in the upper left corner of the Get Info window.

4. From the Edit menu, select Cut (⌘-X) or Clear.

   The icon reverts to its default.

5. Close the Get Info window.

To add a label to an icon

1. Select the icon to which you want to add a label.

2. From the Labels menu, select the label you want to add. For more information, see *Labels Control Panel*.

To remove a label from an icon

1. Select the icon from which you want to remove a label.

2. From the Labels menu, select None.

Note

See also *Labels Control Panel*.

INITs

INITs are now called extensions and are located in the Extensions folder. Some older INITs may not be compatible with System 7.

See also *Extensions Folder*.

Installer

Enables you to install System features onto your Macintosh.

You need to use the Installer if you do any of the following:

- Buy a different Macintosh computer.
- Add a different type of printer.
- Remove a printer.
- Add networking software.

The Installer program updates your Macintosh's System Software so you can use all its features.

For more information, see *Using the Installer* in the Getting Started with System 7 section.

Keyboard Menu

If you have installed more than one language script (such as Arabic or Kanji), the Keyboard menu appears between the Help menu and the Application menu at the right end of the menu bar. Select the language script and keyboard layout you want to use from the Keyboard menu.

Labels Control Panel

Purpose

Enables you to edit the text and color of your labels.

Labels enable you to assign project names and colors to icons on your Macintosh, helping you to identify related files.

To change the contents of the Label menu

1. Open the Labels Control Panel.

2. To change a label's text, click the text you want to change, then type the new text.

3. To change a label's color, double-click the color you want to change, then select the new color from the color wheel.

4. Close the Labels Control Panel.

Note

See also *Find Command*, *Finder*, and *Icons*.

=Memory Control Panel

Purpose

Governs the Macintosh's usage of three features related to memory: the disk cache, virtual memory, and 32-bit addressing.

The Disk Cache

The disk cache stores frequently used information in order to speed up the disk's performance. The disk cache is always on, but you can adjust the amount of RAM used by the disk cache with the buttons in the upper right corner of the Memory Control Panel.

To adjust the disk cache

1. Open the Memory Control Panel (in the Control Panels folder within the System Folder).

2. Examine the amount of memory used for the disk cache.

   By default, System 7 sets the disk cache to 32K for each megabyte of RAM.

3. To adjust the disk cache, type a new value or select an amount from the pop-up menu.

4. Restart the computer.

Virtual Memory

Virtual memory enables you to use a portion of your hard disk as extra RAM. Use virtual memory when you want to work with several large programs or with extremely large documents.

To use virtual memory, your Macintosh must have at least a 68030 processor, or a 68020 with a PMMU chip installed. If your Macintosh does not support virtual memory, System 7 does not display that portion of the control panel.

- The Macintosh Plus, Classic, SE, Portable, and LC do not support virtual memory.

- The Macintosh II, with the optional PMMU, can handle 14M of total memory, including virtual memory, less 1M per NuBus card installed.

- The Macintosh IIx, IIcx, and SE/30 can handle 14M of total memory, including virtual memory, less 1M per NuBus card (whether or not 32-bit addressing is enabled).

- The Macintosh IIci, IIsi, and IIfx can handle 14M of total memory, including virtual memory, less 1M per NuBus card without 32-bit addressing or 1 gigabyte (1000M) with 32-bit addressing.

Virtual memory increases the amount of available memory, but because hard disks operate more slowly than RAM (typically a hundred thousand times more slowly), your computer operates more slowly when you are using virtual memory. If you consistently need virtual memory, consider adding more RAM to your system.

Some programs are incompatible with virtual memory; consult your manuals if you encounter any difficulties.

To enable virtual memory

1. Open the Memory Control Panel (in the Control Panels folder within the System Folder).

2. In the Virtual Memory section of the control panel, click the On button.

3. To adjust the amount of memory, click the up or down arrow.

4. Close the Memory Control Panel.

5. Restart the computer.

To disable virtual memory

1. Open the Memory Control Panel (in the Control Panels folder within the System Folder).

2. In the Virtual Memory section of the control panel, click the Off button.

3. Close the Memory Control Panel.

4. Restart the computer.

32-Bit Addressing

Prior to System 7, the maximum amount of RAM the System could address was 8 megabytes. With System 7's 32-bit addressing option, certain Macintosh models can address 1 gigabyte (1000 megabytes).

To use 32-bit addressing, you must have a Macintosh with 32-bit "clean" ROMs or Connectrix Mode 32 software (distributed free by Apple).

Currently, only the Macintosh IIsi, IIci, and IIfx have 32-bit "clean" ROMs. Connectrix Mode 32 software works with Macintosh II, IIx, IIcx, and SE/30 models and provides them with 128M of RAM.

Some programs are incompatible with 32-bit addressing. Enable the 32-bit addressing option only if you are using more than 8M of RAM or if you want more virtual memory than is available without setting the 32-bit addressing option.

To enable 32-bit addressing

1. Open the Memory Control Panel (in the Control Panels folder within the System Folder).

2. In the 32-bit Addressing section of the control panel, click the On button.

3. Close the Memory Control Panel.

4. Restart the computer.

To disable 32-bit addressing

1. Open the Memory Control Panel (in the Control Panels folder within the System Folder).

2. In the 32-bit Addressing section of the control panel, click the Off button.

3. Close the Memory Control Panel.

4. Restart the computer.

Notes

With System 7, a 2M Macintosh is very cramped. Each font and sound you have takes up memory, as do extensions, File Sharing, and the RAM cache.

For example, File Sharing requires about 250K of RAM. Allocating this much RAM to File Sharing renders a Macintosh with only 2M of RAM nearly useless (except for a few small desk accessories).

If you are running out of memory, remove unused fonts and sounds and disable unneeded extensions by moving them from the Extensions folder and System Folder and restarting the computer. Better yet, install at least 4 megabytes of RAM in your computer—install more RAM if you can.

See also *Extensions Folder* and *System Folder*.

MultiFinder

System 7's Finder includes the features of MultiFinder
from previous System versions: you can use more than
one program at one time, and you can print documents
to a networked laser printer in the background.

If you have never used MultiFinder, browse through the
Before You Install System 7 stack's What's New with
System 7 information (see the Getting Started with
System 7 section).

See also *Finder*.

Network Control Panel

The Network Control Panel is installed only if you have
an EtherTalk or TokenTalk expansion card installed.

If you have either card installed, but the Network
Control Panel is not installed or the EtherTalk or
TokenTalk drivers are not installed, use the Installer's
Customized option to properly install the control panel
or driver. For more information, see *Using the Installer*.

See also *System Folder*.

Network Extension File

For File Sharing to operate properly, the Network
extension file and the File Sharing extension file must
be located in the Extensions folder (within the System
Folder) and the Sharing Setup Control Panel and the
Users & Groups Control Panel must be located in the
Control Panels folder (within the System Folder).

See also *Control Panels Folder*, *Extensions Folder*, *Network Extension File*, *System Folder*, and *Users & Groups Control Panel*.

Preferences Folder

The Preferences folder stores all the preference settings for your applications and for the System itself.

Most applications do not recognize the Preferences folder until upgraded to full System 7 compatibility.

If you delete an application, check the Preferences folder and delete any related preference file as well.

Privacy

Purpose

Ensures that other users do not have casual access to your files.

Privacy guidelines

When you set up shared volumes and folders, keep in mind the following guidelines:

- Share only those volumes and folders you want others to use.

- Organize folders you share in a logical manner.

  If you store all your personal and professional word processing documents in one folder, anyone who has access to any of the professional documents has access to the personal ones as well.

Reorganize folders so that you share files only with those who need to see them.

- Limit access to ensure that other users do not damage information critical to your job.

- If you are under extreme time pressure, disable File Sharing altogether to ensure that your Macintosh's resources are fully available to you.

- Remember that when you store files on other computers, the owners of those computers can revoke your access to those files.

The owner of the Macintosh always has full privileges over whatever is stored on it.

Use caution when you decide to store your information on other computers.

Password guidelines

A password is the only stop sign between your data and another user. Use the following precautions to ensure that your password is secure:

- Do not use single-letter passwords.

- Do not use your name (or anyone else's name) as your password.

- Do not use common passwords. Common passwords include "secret," "user," "guest," "games," and other short words related to the contents of the volume or folder.

- Make your password easy to memorize. If you use a difficult password and need to write it down, you make your password less secure.

- Change your password regularly.

- Change your password if you believe someone else knows it.

File and folder security guidelines

Also consider the following additional security guidelines:

- Remove access for employees who leave the company.

- When an employee transfers to a different area, check that employee's membership in groups and change the groups according to the needs of the new position.

- Limit privileges for Everyone.

- Do not share folders or disks containing sensitive data.

Note

See also *Users & Groups Control Panel.*

Program Linking

Purpose

Enables applications on the same or different computers to communicate with each other.

The applications of other users cannot link to applications on your computer unless you specifically grant permission. Furthermore, you decide which users on the network can use your programs.

Not all programs support Program Linking. Check your manuals before linking programs.

Program Linking possibilities

Suppose that you want to produce a brochure. You need text, graphics, page-layout, and spell-checking capabilities.

You probably would use three programs to create such a brochure: a word processor, a graphics program, and a desktop publishing program—three programs that know how to work together on a limited basis.

What if these programs worked together to share the information in real time? What if your word processing program used stand-alone programs available to any other application for spell-checking and grammar checking?

One of the reasons stand-alone programs remain popular, despite the intentions of those who create multiprogram packages, is that the stand-alone programs offer features not available in packages. With Program Linking, you can take advantage of the greater specialization of such stand-alone programs.

To use Program Linking

Because each program that supports Program Linking does so in a different manner, consult the manuals of your programs to determine whether this feature is available and how to enable it.

To enable others to link to your programs

1. Open the Chooser.

   If the Chooser does not appear on the Apple menu, use the Finder's Find command to locate it.

2. Enable AppleTalk by clicking the Active button (if this button is not already selected).

3. Make sure that you have named your Macintosh. If not, type a name.

4. Open the Sharing Setup Control Panel (in the Control Panels folder within the System Folder).

5. Click the Start button in the Program Linking section of the control panel.

6. Close the Sharing Setup Control Panel.

7. Select the icon of the program you want to share.

8. From the File menu, select Sharing.

9. Select the Allow remote program linking check box.

10. Close the Sharing window.

11. Repeat steps 7 through 10 for each program you want to share.

To disable Program Linking

1. Open the Sharing Setup Control Panel (in the Control Panels folder within the System Folder).

2. Click the Stop button in the Program Linking section of the control panel.

3. Close the Sharing Setup Control Panel.

To disable Program Linking for specified programs

1. In the Finder, select the program for which you want to disable Program Linking.

2. From the File menu, select Sharing.

3. Deselect the Allow remote program linking check box.

4. Close the Sharing window.

5. Repeat steps 1 through 4 for each program for which you want to disable Program Linking.

To enable guests to link to programs

1. Open the Users & Groups Control Panel (in the Control Panels folder within the System Folder).

2. Double-click the Guest icon.

3. Select the Allow guests to link to programs on this Macintosh check box.

4. Close the Guest window.

5. Close the Users & Groups Control Panel.

To enable a specified user to link to programs

1. Open the Users & Groups Control Panel (in the Control Panels folder within the System Folder).

2. Double-click that user's icon.

3. Select the Allow user to link to programs on this Macintosh check box.

4. Close the window.

5. Close the Users & Groups Control Panel.

To disable a user's Program Linking privileges

1. Open the Users & Groups Control Panel (in the Control Panels folder within the System Folder).

2. Double-click that user's icon.

3. Deselect the Allow user to link to programs on this Macintosh check box.

4. Close the window.

5. Close the Users & Groups Control Panel.

Note

See also *Access Privileges* and *IAC*.

Put Away

Purpose

Returns to its previous location a folder or document that you moved to the Desktop or Trash.

In System 7, the Put Away command also can eject disks and other removable media and unmount a shared disk.

To put away a folder or document

1. Select the item you want to return to its previous location.

2. From the File menu, select Put Away.

To eject a disk and remove its icon

1. Select the disk you want to eject.

2. From the File menu, select Put Away.

Remote Access

Purpose

Enables you to connect to your computer from another computer on the network. You then have access to all your files as though you were using your own computer.

To prepare your computer for remote access

1. Your computer must remain on.

2. Open the Sharing Setup Control Panel (in the Control Panels folder within the System Folder).

3. Click the Start button in the File Sharing section of the control panel.

4. Ensure that the Network Identity information is correct.

5. Close the Sharing Setup Control Panel.

6. Open the Users & Groups Control Panel.

7. Double-click the Owner icon (indicated by a bolder outline). This icon's name is your user name.

8. To enable connection from another computer, select the Allow user to connect check box.

9. To see everything while using another computer, select the Allow user to see entire disk check box.

10. Close the Owner window.

11. Close the Users & Groups Control Panel.

You now can connect to your computer from elsewhere on the network.

With a modem and appropriate software, you also can establish the necessary network link from a remote location. Be aware, however, that if you provide this support in your network, others who are not affiliated with your company can access your information.

To establish remote access from another computer

1. Open the Chooser.

   If the Chooser does not appear on the Apple menu, use the Finder's Find command to locate it.

2. Enable AppleTalk by clicking the Active button (if this button is not already selected).

3. Click the AppleShare icon.

4. If your network is divided into zones (zone names appear in the lower left corner of the Chooser window), click the zone in which the computer you want to access resides.

5. Click the name of your computer.

6. Click OK.

   A password dialog box asks you to connect as a guest or a registered user.

7. Type your user name and password.

8. Select the name of the shared disk you want to use. You can type the first part of the name to find it.

   To select more than one volume, hold down the **Shift** or **Command** (⌘) key when selecting subsequent volumes.

9. Click OK.

10. Close the Chooser.

To disable remote access

1. Open the Users & Groups Control Panel (in the Control Panels folder within the System Folder).

2. Deselect the Allow user to connect check box.

   You can no longer access your computer remotely.

Notes

When you enable remote access, anyone who knows your user name and password can connect to your computer and have full access to it. For security, ensure that others do not know your password and disable remote access when you do not need to use it.

See also *File Sharing*, *Privacy*, *Sharing Setup Control Panel*, and *Users & Groups Control Panel*.

Saving and Retrieving Files

Purpose

Enables you to store information now and to retrieve the information later.

New features

System 7 Save and Open dialog boxes look basically the same as in previous System versions; however, they have several new features that make them dramatically different.

- System 7 uses compressed text to display names that exceed 25 characters, enabling your Macintosh to display longer names.

- Alias names appear in italic type.

- The pop-up menu above the list box now includes the Desktop. If you select Desktop from the pop-up menu, the list box displays the volumes and other items on the Desktop.

  In previous System versions, you could select folders and files on the current hard disk only. With System 7, you can open another volume (or any item on the Desktop) just like you open a folder—by double-clicking its name.

- In place of the Drive button, the Open and Save dialog boxes have a Desktop button, which displays in the list box all the items on the Desktop.

- You can use the keyboard to navigate in Save and Save As dialog boxes. In previous System versions, this feature was available only in Open dialog boxes.

Keyboard Shortcuts

Keyboard Shortcut	Effect
Type the name or part of the name of the option.	Selects an item in the active window.
↑	Scrolls up.
↓	Scrolls down.
⌘-↓ or ⌘-O	Opens the selected item.
⌘-↑	Opens the enclosing folder, disk, or volume.
⌘-→	Goes to the next disk or volume.

Keyboard Shortcut	Effect
⌘-←	Goes to the preceding disk or volume.
⌘-D or ⌘-Shift-↑	Goes to the Desktop.
Tab	Moves between the directory listing and file name text box (in Save and Save As dialog boxes).
⌘-N	Creates a new folder. (This shortcut may not work with all programs.)
⌘-Option-O, Option-double-click, or Option-click, Open	Selects the original of the selected alias.

Screen Snapshots

Purpose

Screen snapshots are color pictures of the screen that you can edit, copy, and paste into other programs. Screen snapshots are particularly useful for creating manuals or demonstrating processes.

To create a screen snapshot

1. Arrange the screen as you want it to look in the screen snapshot.

   The mouse pointer appears in the snapshot, so place it in the appropriate location.

2. Press ⌘-Shift-3.

Your Macintosh makes a "camera click" sound.

System 7 names the screen snapshot file Picture 1 (or the next available Picture number) and saves the file outside any folders on your startup disk.

To open a screen snapshot with TeachText

Double-click the screen snapshot's icon.

TeachText opens the snapshot.

To open a screen snapshot with a program other than TeachText

1. Drag the snapshot onto that program's icon. Do not release the mouse button.

If the program can open the snapshot, System 7 highlights the program's icon.

2. Release the mouse button.

The program opens the snapshot as an Untitled document.

Notes

TeachText is a program included with System 7 that enables you to view text documents and screen snapshots.

Previous System versions saved screen snapshots as MacPaint files. System 7 saves screen snapshots in TeachText PICT format.

In addition, previous System versions saved screen snapshots as Screen0 through Screen9, so you could save no more than ten snapshots. System 7 saves screen snapshots as Picture 1, Picture 2, and so on. The number of snapshots you can save is limited only by the available disk space.

Sharing

Purpose

Enables users on different computers to use the same files without using floppy disks to exchange information.

To enable File Sharing for a specific folder or volume

1. Select the icon of the folder or volume for which you want to enable File Sharing.

2. From the File menu, select Sharing.

3. Select the Share this item and its contents check box.

4. Close the Sharing window.

To disable File Sharing for a specific folder or volume

1. Select the icon of the folder or volume for which you want to disable File Sharing.

2. From the File menu, select Sharing.

3. Deselect the Share this item and its contents check box.

4. Close the Sharing window.

Troubleshooting tips

If the Sharing command is dimmed, select a folder, disk, or program you want to share. Then select Sharing from the File menu.

If the Share this item and its contents check box does not appear in the Sharing window, you are already sharing an item that encloses the item you are attempting to share. System 7 considers folders enclosed within shared folders to be shared, so you are trying to share this item twice.

If the Allow remote program linking check box is
dimmed, you have selected an item other than a
program, or the program you selected does not support
remote Program Linking.

Note

See also *Access Privileges* and *Program Linking*.

Sharing Setup Control Panel

Purpose

Enables you to name your Macintosh and its owner and
to start or stop File Sharing and Program Linking.

To name your Macintosh

1. Open the Sharing Setup Control Panel (in the Control
   Panels folder within the System Folder).

2. Enter a name for the owner of the Macintosh (you).

   You use this name when you log in to your
   Macintosh from another computer.

3. Enter a password.

   The password prevents others from connecting to
   your Macintosh as if they were you (with full access).

4. Name your Macintosh.

   This name appears in the Chooser, enabling other
   users to identify your Macintosh.

5. Close the Sharing Setup Control Panel.

To start File Sharing

1. Open the Sharing Setup Control Panel (in the Control
   Panels folder within the System Folder).

2. Click the Start button in the File Sharing section of the control panel.

3. Close the Sharing Setup Control Panel.

To stop File Sharing for all users

1. Open the Sharing Setup Control Panel (in the Control Panels folder within the System Folder).

2. Click the Stop button in the File Sharing section of the control panel.

   System 7 displays the following message:

   ```
   How many minutes until File Sharing
   is disabled?
   ```

3. Enter the number of minutes before System 7 stops File Sharing. Provide enough time for users to save any work in progress.

4. Click OK to stop File Sharing at the specified time or click Cancel to keep File Sharing in effect.

5. Close the Sharing Setup Control Panel.

To disconnect a single user

1. Open the File Sharing Monitor Control Panel (in the Control Panels folder within the System Folder).

2. Select the name of the user you want to disconnect.

3. Click the Disconnect button.

   System 7 displays the following message:

   ```
   How many minutes until user is
   disconnected?
   ```

4. Enter the number of minutes before System 7 disconnects the user. Provide enough time for users to save any work in progress.

5. Click OK.

6. Close the File Sharing Monitor Control Panel.

Note

See also *Access Privileges*, *File Sharing*, *Privacy,* and *Program Linking*.

=| Sounds |

Purpose

Enables you to select the sound that plays whenever your Macintosh "beeps."

Various bulletin board services and user groups provide additional prerecorded sounds, or you can record your own sounds with your Macintosh's microphone.

To install a sound

To install a sound, drag the icon of the sound onto the System file's icon. (You also can drag the sound's icon onto the System Folder's icon.)

To remove an installed sound

1. Open the System file.

2. Locate the sound you want to remove.

3. Drag the sound's icon out of the System file (and out of the System Folder).

To record a sound

1. Open the Sound Control Panel (in the Control Panels folder within the System Folder).

2. Click the icon that represents the sound input method you are using.

For a Macintosh with sound input capability, you usually record sounds with the built-in microphone. Follow steps 3 through 7.

3. Click the Add button.

4. Click the round Record button to start recording.

5. Record your sound, then click the square Stop button.

   You can record for ten seconds.

6. To review your sound, click the triangular Play button.

7. To keep the sound, click Save; otherwise, click Cancel.

For a Macintosh without sound input capability, you need third-party hardware and software, such as Farallon's MacRecorder, to record sounds. In this case, follow the manufacturer's instructions for recording and installing sounds.

To copy and paste a sound into the Scrapbook

1. Open the Sound Control Panel (in the Control Panels folder within the System Folder).

2. Select the sound you want to copy by highlighting its name.

3. From the Edit menu, select Copy.

   or

   Press ⌘-C.

   System 7 copies the sound to the Clipboard.

4. From the Apple menu, select Scrapbook.

5. From the Edit menu, select Paste.

   or

   Press ⌘-V.

   System 7 pastes the sound to the Scrapbook.

6. To hear the sound, click the Play Sound button.

7. Close the Scrapbook.

8. Close the Sound Control Panel.

Note

See also *System File*.

Startup Items Folder

Purpose

Contains items that System 7 opens at startup.

In System 7, the Startup Items folder can open documents as well as applications. Because the startup items are in a folder, you can review and change the items easily.

In previous System versions, you used the Set Startup command to select the applications opened at startup.

To select items to open at startup

1. Select the item or items you want to open at startup.

2. Drag those items into the Startup Items folder (in the System Folder).

   At startup, System 7 alphabetically opens the applications along with their documents, then alphabetically opens all other types of items in the Startup Items folder.

3. To see the effect of the changes, restart the computer.

   Otherwise the changes take effect the next time you start the computer.

To prevent items from opening at startup

To prevent items from opening at startup, drag the icons of those items out of the Startup Items folder (and out of the System Folder).

The changes take effect the next time you start the computer.

Notes

Including desk accessories, folders, or control panels in the Startup Items folder slows the startup process. When a folder or control panel follows a desk accessory alphabetically, the Finder's icon flashes in the Application menu. You then must switch to the Finder to load the remaining items in the Startup Items folder.

See also *Application Menu* and *System Folder*.

Stationery Pads

Purpose

Creates document templates that you can reuse.

You can use Stationery Pads within any application (although only System 7 Savvy applications recognize that a Stationery Pad is a read-only template).

To save a Stationery Pad from within an application

When you save the file (by using the normal procedure for that application), select the Stationery Pad check box in the Save dialog box.

To save a document as a Stationery Pad from within an application, that application must support Stationery Pads. If no Stationery Pad check box appears, the application does not yet support Stationery Pads.

To change a document into a Stationery Pad

1. Select the document you want to change into a Stationery Pad.

2. From the File menu, select Get Info.

   or

   Press ⌘-**I**.

3. Select the Stationery Pad check box.

4. Close the Get Info window.

   The document's icon changes to the Stationery Pad's icon.

To determine a Stationery Pad's creator

1. Select the Stationery Pad's icon.

2. From the File menu, select Get Info.

   or

   Press ⌘-**I**.

   The Get Info window displays the file's information, including its creator.

3. Close the Get Info window.

To use a Stationery Pad

Double-click the Stationery Pad's icon.

The application creates a new, Untitled document with all the features (including any text or graphics) of the Stationery Pad.

For example, you can create a letterhead document and save it as a Stationery Pad. Whenever you want to write a letter, double-click the Stationery Pad's icon. The application opens a new, Untitled document with the letterhead in place.

Notes

When you create a Stationery Pad from a document, the new Stationery Pad has the same information in the Get Info window as the document.

All Stationery Pads have the same icon, regardless of their creators. Aliases of Stationery Pads also have the Stationery Pad icon.

If you open a Stationery Pad document with an application that does not support Stationery Pads, the application may ignore the fact that a Stationery Pad is a template and enable you to overwrite the Stationery Pad. An application that supports Stationery Pads should open a new, Untitled document.

See also *System Folder*.

System 7 Hotline

Apple operates a System 7 Hotline for users who have questions about or difficulties with System 7.

Every System 7 package includes a card with a unique ID number. You can use this ID number to obtain 90 days of free technical support. The toll-free number is also in the upgrade kit.

If you did not purchase the upgrade kit, you can get technical support from Apple for $2.00 per minute by calling (900) 535-2775.

Apple also provides automated help 24 hours a day, 7 days a week for all System 7 users. For automated System 7 help, call (408) 257-7700.

System 7 Savvy

System 7 Savvy is an Apple label which indicates that an application meets the following System 7 compatibility criteria:

- The application supports multitasking. The application does not use the entire processing capacity of your Macintosh, but enables other applications to operate in the background. The application should operate in the foreground and in the background, as well as support background processing.

- The application is "32-bit clean," which means that it can operate correctly when more than 8M of RAM is installed.

- The application supports the Publish and Subscribe features. With Publish and Subscribe, applications can share data as if using a real-time Clipboard.

- The application imposes no font size limitations. Previous System versions did not support fonts larger than 127 points. System 7 Savvy applications must support font sizes from 1 to 32,000 points in single-point increments.

- The application provides Balloon Help, which shows users how to use the application.

- The application supports AppleShare.

  System 7 also offers File Sharing, which is similar to AppleShare. File Sharing enables users to access data on other computers on the network without additional software.

- The application supports Stationery Pads. Stationery Pads are a universal, read-only document template which enable users to create new documents without repeating common text or graphics.

Several applications have supported templates of
their own design for years; however, you can use
Stationery Pads with any System 7 Savvy application.

System File

The System 7 System file contains fonts, sounds,
language definitions, and keyboard layouts. Desk
accessories are no longer part of the System file.

This entry presents the features of the System file that
are new to System 7 and not covered in another section.
The features covered in other sections are referenced in
the Notes.

To review which fonts are installed

1. Double-click the System file (in the System Folder).

   The System file's window displays the contents of
   the System file, including the installed fonts.

2. Review which fonts are installed.

   You can use the Finder's View menu to switch from
   icon view to a list view.

3. Close the System file's window.

To review which sounds are installed

1. Double-click the System file (in the System Folder).

   The System file's window displays the contents of
   the System file, including the installed sounds.

2. Review which sounds are installed.

   You can use the Finder's View menu to switch from
   icon view to a list view.

3. Close the System file's window.

Notes

Desk accessories are no longer part of the System file.
System 7 initially stores desk accessories in the Apple
Menu Items folder, but you can store and use desk
accessories almost anywhere.

See also *Desk Accessories*, *Fonts*, *Sounds*, and *System
Folder*.

System Folder

Purpose

Contains the items necessary for the Macintosh to
operate.

In System 7, the System Folder contains the Apple
Menu Items folder, the Control Panels folder, and the
Extensions folder as well as folders that were in the
System Folder of previous System versions.

To move items into the System Folder

To move items into the System Folder, simply drag their
icons onto the System Folder icon.

When you place an item in the System Folder that
probably should go into one of the folders inside the
System Folder (for example, the Control Panels folder),
System 7 displays a message that asks whether to put the
item in that folder.

If you click OK, System 7 places these items in the
appropriate folder in the System Folder.

To move documents or applications into the System Folder

Because the System Folder does not know where to
place documents or applications, place them directly into

the appropriate folder inside the System Folder. Usually, you place documents or applications in the Startup Items folder or the Apple Menu Items folder.

To place a document or application in both the Startup Items folder and the Apple Menu Items folder, create an alias for the item, and then place one icon in one folder and one in the other folder.

To remove items from the System Folder

To remove items from the System Folder, simply drag them out of the System Folder. Make sure that you also drag the items out of any folders contained within the System Folder.

Note

See also *Aliases*, *Apple Menu Items Folder*, and *Startup Items Folder*.

System Memory

Purpose

System Memory is the RAM inside your computer.

To see how much memory you have available

To see how much memory you have available, select About This Macintosh from the Apple menu.

To clear fragmented memory

Each program you open reserves memory for itself. If you open and close several programs, your Macintosh has less and less memory available in a consecutive block, although it may have several smaller blocks available. Consequently, a program may not find sufficient memory to operate, even if enough memory is available.

If your computer slows down, or you cannot open a program that your Macintosh should have enough memory to open, quit all the programs you have open, and then reopen each one. This technique may clear some memory. If the cleared memory is still insufficient, restart the computer and try again.

To change the amount of memory an application reserves

1. Select the icon of the program whose memory usage you want to change.

   You can change the amount of memory an application uses only when the program is on an unlocked disk or volume.

2. From the File menu, select Get Info.

   or

   Press ⌘-I.

   The Finder displays the Get Info window. In the lower right corner of the window, Get Info displays two values:

   Suggested size is the minimum amount of RAM to reserve for the program, as specified by the developer.

   Current size is the amount of RAM the program reserves for itself when you use it. (If you are working with a very large document, you may need to increase the Current size.)

3. Enter a new value for Current size.

   Type a number that is at least as large as the Suggested size; otherwise, the program may run very slowly or not at all. If you enter a number that is too large, however, you may not be able to run other applications at the same time.

4. Close the Get Info window.

Notes

The more memory you have, the less you need to worry about managing it. Although it is possible to use System 7 with only 2M of RAM, System 7 operates much more smoothly if you have at least 4M of RAM.

Do not spend a lot of money buying more than 8M of RAM, however, unless you are sure that you really need that much memory and that the programs with which you intend to use the additional memory are compatible with 32-bit addressing.

See also *Memory Control Panel* and *Virtual Memory*.

Trash

Purpose

Deletes files. You also can use the Trash to eject disks or to discard the icons of disks you have ejected.

System 7 changes

With System 7, the Trash no longer empties when you launch an application or restart or shut down the Macintosh. To empty the Trash, you must select Empty Trash from the Special menu.

You also can make aliases of the Trash and move them to anywhere on the Desktop. Dragging an icon to an alias of the Trash is the same as dragging the icon to the original Trash.

System 7 does not display a warning when you drag locked items to the Trash, but does display a warning when you try to empty the Trash. As with previous System versions, the Trash does not remove locked items.

You now can eject disks and discard their icons by selecting Put Away from the File menu as well as by dragging the disks to the Trash.

To move the Trash icon

With System 7, when you move the Trash icon, it remains in its new position, even after you empty it. With previous System versions, the Trash icon returned to the lower right corner of the Desktop when you emptied it.

To move items from the Trash to their preceding location

1. Double-click the Trash icon to see the contents of the Trash.

2. Select the item or items you want to move from the Trash.

3. From the File menu, select Put Away.

To put items with the same name into the Trash

If you drag an item to the Trash, and the Trash already contains an item with the same name, the Finder renames the existing item in the Trash, and moves the second item into the Trash as well.

System 7 renames the files just as if it were copying them. If the Trash contains a file named Fred, and you moved another Fred file into the Trash, System 7 renames the original Fred file as Fred copy and moves the second Fred file into the Trash.

To turn off the Trash warning temporarily

When you empty the Trash, System 7 displays the number of items you are discarding and the amount of space these items occupy.

To disable this feature temporarily, hold down the
Option key while selecting Empty Trash from the
Special menu.

To disable the Trash warning

1. Select the Trash icon.

2. From the File menu, select Get Info.

   or

   Press ⌘-I.

3. Deselect the Warn before emptying check box.

4. Close the Get Info window.

To enable the Trash warning

1. Select the Trash icon.

2. From the File menu, select Get Info.

   or

   Press ⌘-I.

3. Select the Warn before emptying check box.

4. Close the Get Info window.

To discard items from removable media

If you move items from a floppy disk (or other
removable media, such as a cartridge drive) into the
Trash and then eject the disk, those items no longer
appear in the Trash but are not permanently discarded.
When you reinsert that disk (or cartridge, and so on), the
discarded items reappear in the Trash.

System 7 does, however, permanently discard any items
from 400K disks when you empty the Trash.

To recover rescued files

The Rescued Items folder, located in the Trash after a System crash, contains recovered temporary files in use when your Macintosh crashed. You may be able to reconstruct some of your work from these temporary files.

The Rescued Items folder also may appear if you did not use Shut Down properly.

Caution

If you are sharing another user's disk or folder on the network, and you drag an item from the shared disk to your Trash, the item does not move to the Trash on the host computer. If you select Empty Trash from the Special menu, however, System 7 permanently discards that item from the host computer.

Similarly, you cannot tell whether someone using your disk or folders is dragging items to his or her Trash (and may be about to discard them permanently). You can, however, prevent this situation by limiting access.

Note

See also *Access Privileges* and *Put Away*.

TrueType Fonts

TrueType is a new font technology created by Apple that enables you to display or print fonts accurately at any size on an output device of any resolution, such as screens, StyleWriters, and laser printers. TrueType is compatible with System 7 only.

TrueType fonts, also called *variable-sized fonts* or *outline fonts*, do not require separate files for screen and printer fonts. Although TrueType fonts are not a replacement for PostScript fonts, they offer many of the same advantages as PostScript fonts used with Adobe Type Manager.

Benefits of TrueType include the following:

- TrueType fonts are scalable fonts that you can display or print in any size. You have only one font file for multiple font sizes.

- TrueType fonts provide outline font support in all applications.

- TrueType fonts are compatible with existing font definitions; you can use multiple varieties of fonts in one document without problems.

- Because TrueType is a published specification, font vendors can create their own TrueType fonts.

- Microsoft has announced plans to support TrueType in future versions of OS/2 and Windows for compatibility across platforms.

You can recognize TrueType fonts by their icons (which show several sizes of the letter *A*) and by the absence of a font size after the font name. Icons for fixed-size fonts have only one letter *A* and include the size after the font name.

When you double-click a font's icon, System 7 displays text set in that font. TrueType font icons display text in three sizes, but fixed-size fonts display text in the designated size only.

If you have PostScript screen fonts and TrueType fonts of the same name in your System file, the Macintosh lists only one entry for these fonts on the Font menu.

The character widths of TrueType fonts and PostScript fonts are different. When both types of font exist, the application, not the System, determines which font it uses to set the text. Until you print the document, you do not know which font the application used. To avoid unexpected results, avoid having TrueType and PostScript fonts of the same name in your System file.

See also *Fonts*.

Users & Groups Control Panel

Purpose

Enables you to define users and groups of users who use your computer from their computers and to set or deny access for those users and groups.

Users

A *user* is a person who uses your computer from another computer on your network. When you define a user, that person becomes a *registered user* of your computer.

A *guest* is any person who uses your computer from another computer on your network, but is not a registered user.

Because every person on your network can use your computer as a guest, you do not need to make every person who uses your computer a registered user; define only those users to whom you want to assign special access privileges.

To define a user

1. Open the Users & Groups Control Panel (in the Control Panels folder within the System Folder).

2. From the File menu, select New User.

   or

   Press ⌘-N.

3. Type a name for the new user.

4. Double-click that user's icon to change the settings.

5. Select or deselect the Allow user to connect check box.

   This check box determines whether that user can connect to your Macintosh.

6. Type a password in the upper right corner of the window. Be sure to give the password to the user.

7. Select or deselect the Allow user to change password check box.

   You can always change the user's password; this check box determines whether the user can change the password.

8. Select or deselect the Allow user to link to programs on this Macintosh check box.

   This check box enables or disables Program Linking for the user.

9. Close the user's window.

10. Close the Users & Groups Control Panel or define additional users or groups.

To deny access to a specific user

1. Open the Users & Groups Control Panel (in the Control Panels folder within the System Folder).

2. Double-click the icon of the user that you want to deny access.

3. Deselect the Allow user to connect check box.

4. Close the user's window.

5. Close the Users & Groups Control Panel or make additional changes.

To deny access to guest users

1. Open the Users & Groups Control Panel (in the Control Panels folder within the System Folder).

2. Double-click the Guest icon.

3. Deselect the Allow user to connect check box.

4. Close the Guest window.

5. Close the Users & Groups Control Panel or make additional changes.

To deny remote access to yourself

1. Open the Users & Groups Control Panel (in the Control Panels folder within the System Folder).

2. Double-click your user icon.

3. Deselect the Allow user to connect check box.

   Denying access to yourself does not prevent you from using your Macintosh from your Macintosh, but does prevent you from using your Macintosh from another Macintosh on the network.

4. Close your window.

5. Close the Users & Groups Control Panel or make additional changes.

Groups

A *group* is a set of users. Because you can change membership in a group, controlling access with groups is easier than adding and deleting users from folders. Groups cannot contain other groups.

To define a group

1. Open the Users & Groups Control Panel (in the Control Panels folder within the System Folder).

2. From the File menu, select New Group.

3. Type a name for that group.

   Note that users cannot see the names of the groups they do or do not belong to.

4. Close the Users & Groups Control Panel or define other groups.

To add users to a group

1. Open the Users & Groups Control Panel (in the Control Panels folder within the System Folder).

2. Select the user or users you want to add to the group.

3. Drag the icon(s) for the user(s) onto the group's icon.

4. Close the Users & Groups Control Panel or make additional changes.

To see which users are members of a group

1. Open the Users & Groups Control Panel (in the Control Panels folder within the System Folder).

2. Double-click the icon of the group whose membership you want to see.

3. After reviewing the group's membership, close the group's window.

4. Close the Users & Groups Control Panel or make additional changes.

To remove a user from a group

1. Open the Users & Groups Control Panel (in the Control Panels folder within the System Folder).

2. Double-click the icon of the group from which you want to delete users.

3. Drag the user(s) you want to remove from the group to the Trash (or to the Trash's alias).

   This procedure removes the user(s) from that group, but does not affect membership in other groups or access privileges.

4. Close the group's window.

5. Close the Users & Groups Control Panel or make additional changes.

To remove a user or a group

1. Open the Users & Groups Control Panel (in the Control Panels folder within the System Folder).

2. Drag the user or group you want to remove to the Trash (or to the Trash's alias).

When deleting a user, this procedure revokes their access privileges, any group memberships, and any ownership of folders or volumes.

When deleting a group, this procedure removes the users from the group, but does not affect the users themselves. This procedure also revokes any access privileges or ownership of folders or volumes.

3. Close the Users & Groups Control Panel or make additional changes.

Notes

If you change a folder's ownership to another user or group and then delete that user or group, the folder's ownership reverts to you.

See also *Access Privileges*.

Views Control Panel

Purpose

Enables you to modify the way your Finder windows appear. As with previous System versions, you can display your directories by icon or by list.

To set the display font and size

1. Open the Views Control Panel (in the Controls Panels folder within the System Folder).

2. From the pop-up menu of fonts, select the font you want to use.

3. From the pop-up menu of font sizes, select the size you want to use.

4. Close the Views Control Panel.

To select a straight or staggered grid

1. Display files by icon.

2. Open the Views Control Panel (in the Controls Panels folder within the System Folder).

3. To select a straight grid, click the Straight Grid button.

   To select a staggered grid, click the Staggered Grid button.

4. To force icons to snap to the grid whenever you move them, select the Always snap to grid check box.

   To cancel this option, deselect the Always snap to grid check box.

5. Close the Views Control Panel.

To show disk information

1. Open the Views Control Panel (in the Controls Panels folder within the System Folder).

2. Select the Show disk info in header check box.

   In the top of each window, System 7 displays the number of items contained in the window, the total used space on the current disk, and the total free space on the current disk.

   To cancel this option, deselect the Show disk info in header check box.

3. Close the Views Control Panel.

To calculate folder sizes

1. Open the Views Control Panel (in the Controls Panels folder within the System Folder).

2. Select the Calculate folder sizes check box.

   Note that if the folder contains many items, selecting this option seriously degrades performance.

To cancel this option, deselect the Calculate folder
sizes check box.

3. Close the Views Control Panel.

To determine a folder's size without calculating the folder size

1. Select the folder whose size you want to know.

2. From the File menu, select Get Info.

3. After you review the information, close the Get Info
   window.

To adjust icon sizes in list views

1. Open the Views Control Panel (in the Controls Panels
   folder within the System Folder).

2. To set the size of the icon displayed in list views,
   click the appropriate button from the series of three.

3. Close the Views Control Panel.

To adjust information displayed in list views

1. Open the Views Control Panel (in the Controls Panels
   folder within the System Folder).

2. To display or hide file sizes, select or deselect the
   Show size check box.

3. To display or hide file types, select or deselect the
   Show kind check box.

4. To display or hide file labels, select or deselect the
   Show labels check box.

5. To display or hide the date each file was last modified, select or deselect the Show date check box.

6. To display or hide the file version numbers, select or
   deselect the Show version check box.

7. To display or hide the file comments, select or deselect the Show comments check box.

8. Close the Views Control Panel.

Note

See also *Fonts*, *Get Info*, *Icons*, and *Labels Control Panel*.

Virtual Memory

Virtual memory is a portion of the hard disk that is set aside as extra RAM. When your Macintosh runs out of memory, it uses the virtual memory as the additional RAM it needs. To enable or disable virtual memory, use the Memory Control Panel.

See *Memory Control Panel*.

FINDER MENU REFERENCE

This section lists all the items on the Finder's menus and provides a brief description of the item or a reference to related entries in the Command Reference.

Apple Menu

Lists items stored in the Apple Menu Items folder.

About this Macintosh

Opens a window that lists the System Software version, the amount of total memory, and the amount of available memory.

In addition, the window displays a list of the currently
open applications, the amount of memory each application reserves, and a thermometer that indicates what
portion of its reserved memory each application is
currently using.

To adjust the amount of memory reserved by an
application, see *Get Info*.

To close the window, click the close box in the upper
left corner of the window.

Other Apple Menu items

Lists in alphabetical order the items stored in your Apple
Menu Items folder.

To change the contents of the Apple menu, see *Apple
Menu Items Folder*.

For information on desk accessories on the Apple menu,
see *Desk Accessories*.

Alarm Clock

Enables you to set the Macintosh's time and date; also
enables you to set an alarm.

When the alarm rings, your Macintosh beeps and the
alarm clock flashes on top of the Apple menu icon.

If you have a screen-saver program (such as After Dark)
installed, the alarm clock moves across the screen and
displays the message

```
Please wake up!
```

To turn off the alarm warning, open and close the Alarm
Clock.

You also can set the date and time via the General
Controls Control Panel.

Calculator

Enables you to use the keyboard or mouse to set up
calculations.

Because the calculator has no Clear Entry button, use the Note Pad to set up complex calculations: enter text in the Note Pad, copy the text, and then paste the text into the calculator. The calculator then displays the answer.

Chooser

Enables you to select a printer or the remote computer to which you want to connect and to enable or disable AppleTalk.

See also *Accessing Other Computers*.

Control Panels

Displays a window where you can adjust the settings of all installed Control Panels.

See also *Control Panels*, *File Sharing Monitor Control Panel*, *Labels Control Panel*, *Memory Control Panel*, *Sharing Setup Control Panel*, *Users & Groups Control Panel*, and *Views Control Panel*.

Key Caps

Enables you to see what keys produce specific characters.

To see the keyboard in a specific font, select that font from the Key Caps menu. (The Key Caps menu lists all installed fonts.)

Press the **Shift**, **Option**, and **Control** keys (individually and in combination) to see what keystroke combination are available in the font you select from the Key Caps menu (Chicago is the default font).

Note Pad

A small eight-page pad where you can enter, edit, copy, cut, and paste text.

Puzzle

A simple game.

Scrapbook

Enables you to store text, graphics, and sounds.

File Menu

Enables you to open applications and print documents.

New Folder

Creates a new folder (named Untitled folder) in the current Finder window.

Open

Opens the selected disk or folder, enabling you to see the contents. Opens the selected application or document, enabling you to edit, revise, and create documents.

You also can double-click an icon to open that item.

Print

Enables you to select one or more documents (from one or more applications) and to print the documents without first opening their applications.

Close Window

Closes the current window.

You also can click the close box to close the window.

Get Info

Gets information about a disk, folder, document, or
application. Enables you to change an item's icon,
lock or unlock a document or application, and set an
application's memory usage.

See *Get Info*, *Icons*, and *Stationery Pads*.

Sharing

Shares the selected folder or disk for use by others on
the network and sets the privileges for users and guests
on the network. Also enables you to share applications
across the network.

See *Access Privileges*, *File Sharing*, *File Sharing
Monitor Control Panel*, *Program Linking*, *Sharing Setup
Control Panel*, and *Users & Groups Control Panel*.

Duplicate

Copies a folder, document, or application. A duplicate of
the file Fred is named Fred copy.

Make Alias

Creates a copy of an item's icon that you can put elsewhere (such as in the Apple Menu Items folder) and use
as though it were the original icon.

See *Aliases* and *Apple Menu Items Folder*.

Put Away

Moves selected items on the Desktop or in the Trash to
their preceding locations. Also, ejects and removes the
icon of floppy disks or disconnects and removes the icon
of network disks.

See *Put Away*.

Find

Finds the first item that matches the specified criteria.

See *Find Command*.

Find Again

Finds the next item that matches the specified criteria.

See *Find Command*.

Page Setup

Enables you to set the page specifications for printing.

Print Window

Prints the contents of the current window to the current printer (set the current printer with the Chooser on the Apple menu) according to the specifications in Page Setup.

Edit

Supports basic editing functions.

Undo

Undoes your preceding action.

Cut

Removes selected text or graphics and copies it to the Clipboard (a storage area available to all applications).

Copy

Copies the selected text or graphics to the Clipboard (a storage area available to all applications).

Paste

Pastes the contents of the Clipboard into the current document at the specified location.

Clear

Removes the selected text or graphics without copying it to the Clipboard.

Select All

Selects all items in the current document.

Show Clipboard

Shows the contents of the Clipboard.

View Menu

Enables you to change the manner in which you view Finder windows.

See also *Views Control Panel*.

by Small Icon

Displays a small icon and the icon's name for each item in the current window.

by Icon

Displays a full-size icon and the icon's name for each item in the current window.

by Name

Displays the items in the current window sorted in alphabetical order by name.

by Size

Displays the items in the current window sorted in descending order by size.

by Kind

Displays items in the current window sorted in alphabetical order by type of item (alias, application, document, system extension, and so on).

by Label

Displays items in the current window sorted in label order.

The Labels Control Panel determines label order. Items without a label appear last, although None (for no label) appears first on the Label menu.

See *Labels Control Panel*.

by Date

Displays items in the current window sorted in order by the date last modified. The most recently modified items appear first.

Label Menu

Displays the customized list of labels you can associate with files.

None

Removes a label associated with an icon and returns the icon's color to its default.

Other Label menu items

Selects the label and colors the icon.

To edit the descriptions and colors of the Label menu, see *Labels Control Panel*.

Special Menu

Enables you to perform specialized tasks, including turning off your Macintosh.

Clean Up

Aligns the icons to an invisible grid.

See *Clean Up* and *Views Control Panel*.

Empty Trash

Empties the contents of the Trash.

Eject Disk

Ejects the selected disk.

Erase Disk

Erases the selected disk. You cannot erase the startup disk.

Restart

Starts your Macintosh.

Before turning off the power to your Macintosh, always select Restart or Shut Down (to ensure that your Macintosh completes any important tasks).

Shut Down

Prepares your Macintosh to be turned off. On some Macintosh models, selecting this item also turns off the Macintosh.

Before turning off the power to your Macintosh, always select Restart or Shut Down (to ensure that your Macintosh completes any important tasks).

Help Menu

Enables you to get more information about items.

The Help menu appears at the right end of the menu bar; its icon is a word balloon that encloses a question mark.

See *Help Menu*.

About Balloon Help

Provides more information about activating and using Balloon Help.

Show (Hide) Balloons

Enables you to show or hide Balloon Help.

If you enable Balloon Help, this menu item is Hide Balloons. Otherwise, this menu item is Show Balloons.

Finder Shortcuts

Provides information about using the Finder.

See *Finder* and the Keyboard Shortcuts section.

KEYBOARD SHORTCUTS

This section provides a reference to common keyboard shortcuts.

Finder, Chooser, and Dialog Box Shortcuts

Shortcut	Effect
⌘-D	Desktop; selects the Desktop button.
⌘-→	Next drive; selects the next available drive.
⌘-←	Preceding drive; selects the preceding drive.
Tab	In Save As dialog boxes, toggles between the scrolling file list and the file name text box. The active box has a black border.

When the file name text box is active, the arrow keys move the cursor within the text box, and you can type a file name. In System 7, you can use Copy and Paste with your file name. If the application you are using does not support selecting Copy or Paste from the Edit menu, you can use the Command key equivalents (⌘-C and ⌘-V).

When the scrolling file list is active, you can type a letter or letters to go to that section of the list (see *a* and *abc* later in this list), then use the arrow keys to navigate.

Shortcut	Effect
	Note that System 7's use of **Tab** is unlike previous System versions, in which pressing **Tab** selected the Drive button.
⌘-↓	When you select a folder in an Open or Save dialog box, opens the folder and displays its contents.
⌘-↑	Closes the folder and displays the contents of its enclosing folder or volume.
a	Moves to the first item starting with the letter *a*. If no such item exists, moves to the next item in the list after the letter *a*. If the letter *a* is after the last item, moves to the last item in the list.
abc	Moves to the first item starting with the letters *abc*. If no such item exists, moves to the next item in the list after the letters *abc*. If the letters *abc* are after the last item, moves to the last item in the list.

Application Shortcuts

Most of the following commands are available in most applications, but the specific commands available do vary slightly from program to program.

Shortcut	Command
⌘-C	Copy
⌘-V	Paste

Shortcut	Command
⌘-X	Cut
⌘-B	Bold (or, in some applications, Clear)
⌘-P	Print
⌘-A	Select All
⌘-O	Open
⌘-N	New
⌘-Q	Quit

GLOSSARY

The Glossary lists key terms used throughout this book and provides references to related Glossary and Command Reference entries.

active application

The application you are currently using. Many applications can be running (depending on available memory), but only one application can be active.

alias

A copy of an icon that acts exactly like the original icon. You can recognize aliases by their italic titles (which initially include the word *Alias*).

See also *Aliases* in the Command Reference.

AppleTalk

A network of computers, devices, cables, and software that operate according to Apple's guidelines on sharing information. The most common AppleTalk network consists of several Apple computers sharing a LaserWriter.

Application menu

The menu that tells you which applications are running and enables you to switch between applications. The Application menu also enables you to show and hide applications on the Desktop.

See also *Application Menu* in the Command Reference.

background

Any application that is not the active application is "in the background." The active application is "in the foreground."

See also *background processing* and *foreground*.

background processing

Applications in the background can use part of the computer's time to fulfill their tasks, such as copying files in the Finder or printing with Print Monitor.

See also *background* and *foreground*.

balloon

Also called *Balloon Help*. A comic-book balloon shape that displays information on how to use your computer. You turn on or off balloons via the Help menu.

See also *Help Menu* in the Command Reference.

bit-mapped font

A font available in only one size. When you use this typeface in a different size, your computer enlarges or reduces the font by a method that causes jagged edges.

See also *font* in the Glossary and *Fonts* in the Command Reference.

cache

See *disk cache* and *memory cache*.

Chooser

A desk accessory that enables you to select printers, enable or disable AppleTalk, and so on.

close box

The box you use to close a window. The close box is the small box in the upper left corner of the window (at the left end of the title bar).

See also *Windows* in the Macintosh Basics section.

desk accessories

Small application programs with limited functions that perform very specific tasks. The desk accessories included with System 7 include the Alarm Clock, Chooser, and Scrapbook.

Previous System versions stored desk accessories in suitcases, installed them in the System File, and placed them on the Apple menu. With System 7, you treat desk accessories like any other application.

See also *Desk Accessories* in the Command Reference.

Desktop

The "desk" or background on which all folders open and all applications operate.

disk cache

A portion of the computer's memory that is an exact copy of frequently used places on the disk, such as the disk's directory.

Without a disk cache, the computer searches for each file as though it had never used the file before. With a cache, the computer looks first in the cache, then on the disk. Because accessing the computer's memory is hundreds of thousands of times faster than accessing a hard disk, the time savings can be dramatic.

See also *Memory Control Panel* in the Command Reference.

driver

Also called *device driver*. A System extension that tells the computer how to find and communicate with an external object, such as a printer or disk drive.

Although many users think of drivers as part of the computer, disk drives and keyboards also require drivers (although these drivers are part of the System). Common drivers include the ImageWriter and LaserWriter extension files.

To install a driver, drag its icon into the System Folder.

Easy Access

Easy Access is the name of a control panel that enables you to set mouse keys, slow keys, and sticky keys. These features help those who have difficulty using the mouse or keyboard to better use their computer.

See also *mouse keys*, *slow keys*, and *sticky keys* in the Glossary and *Easy Access Control Panel* in the Command Reference.

edition

A portion of a document that you have published. An edition is a file separate from the original document that System 7 updates any time you update the corresponding portion of the original document. Other documents can *subscribe* to the edition; when System 7 updates the edition, it also updates any subscribers.

See also *publisher* and *subscriber* in the Glossary and *Automatic Updating* in the Command Reference.

extension

See *System extension*.

file server

A computer using software that enables other users to store and retrieve files on that computer's disks.

fixed-size font

See *bit-mapped font*.

font

Technically, a font is a set of characters that appear in the same typeface, style (bold, italic, and so on), and size. In Macintosh usage, however, the term means any

set of characters in the same typeface and style,
regardless of size.

See also *TrueType font* in the Glossary and *Fonts* and
TrueType Fonts in the Command Reference.

foreground

The active application is "in the foreground" (at the
front of the computer's attention). All other applications
are "in the background."

See also *background* and *background processing*.

INIT

See *System extension*.

Installer

A program that installs or updates your Macintosh
software. The Installer also enables you to install new
options if your hardware changes.

See also *Using the Installer* in the Getting Started with
System 7 section and *Installer* in the Command
Reference.

label

A short phrase and a color you can assign to an icon (via
the Finder's Label menu) to make the icon easier to
identify. The label's text appears in list views of Finder
windows; the color appears in both list and icon views.
You can edit label text and colors with the Labels
Control Panel.

See also *Labels Control Panel* in the Command
Reference.

LocalTalk

The cables and connectors (on the back of your
Macintosh) that connect Macintoshes in an AppleTalk
network.

See also *AppleTalk*.

memory cache

Memory dedicated to increasing the efficiency (and, therefore, speed) of your computer.

menu

A list of related commands (actions your computer can perform). The menu names appear in the menu bar at the top of the screen.

See also *Menus* in the Macintosh Basics section.

mouse

A device that enables you to point to and select various items on-screen. When you move the mouse across a flat surface, the Macintosh translates your movements to the mouse pointer on-screen.

See also *Mouse Basics* in the Macintosh Basics section.

mouse button

The button on the top of the mouse. You use the mouse button to click, double-click, Shift-click, and drag items.

See also *Mouse Basics* in the Macintosh Basics section.

mouse keys

An Easy Access feature that enables you to use the numeric keypad keys in place of the mouse. Although primarily designed for users who have difficulty using the mouse, mouse keys can be quite handy for fine control in graphics programs.

See also *Easy Access*, *sticky keys*, and *slow keys* in the Glossary and *Easy Access Control Panel* in the Command Reference.

network

A collection of computers, cables, and peripheral devices (such as printers) that communicate according to defined rules (called a *protocol*).

For example, AppleTalk networks communicate according to the rules of Apple's AFP specification.

publisher

A document that contains information, stored in an *edition*, that System 7 automatically updates in other documents, called *subscribers*.

See also *edition* and *subscriber* in the Glossary and *Automatic Updating* in the Command Reference.

RAM

Acronym for Random-Access Memory, the memory your Macintosh uses to operate.

resources

Icons, cursors, fonts, menus, and windows (among other items) are resources an application uses to interact with the user. An application stores the resources together.

ROM

Acronym for Read-Only Memory, the memory to which your Macintosh refers for instructions on such tasks as opening windows, displaying fonts, communicating with the floppy disk drive, and starting the computer.

scroll arrows

The arrows that appear at both ends of a scroll bar.

See also *scroll bar*.

scroll bar

A grey bar at the right or bottom (or both) of a window that you use to change the view in the window. Scroll bars appear whenever the window contains more items than you can view on-screen at one time.

See also *scroll arrows* and *thumb* in the Glossary and *Windows* in the Macintosh Basics section.

shared disk

A disk used by more than one computer to store information.

size box

The box you use to resize a window. The size box is the box within a box in the lower right corner of the window (between the scroll arrows).

See also *Windows* in the Macintosh Basics section.

slow keys

An Easy Access feature that prevents accidental keystrokes by requiring you to press keys for a certain duration before the computer accepts the keystroke.

See also *Easy Access*, *mouse keys*, and *sticky keys* in the Glossary and *Easy Access Control Panel* in the Command Reference.

Stationery Pad

A document template that enables you to create a predefined form, and then use the template to create completed forms. Stationery Pads work with any System 7 Savvy application.

See also *Stationery Pads* in the Command Reference.

sticky keys

An Easy Access feature that enables you to type combination keystrokes without pressing the keys at the same time.

See also *Easy Access*, *mouse keys*, and *slow keys* in the Glossary and *Easy Access Control Panel* in the Command Reference.

subscriber

A document that uses information from an edition. When you change the document that publishes the edition, System 7 automatically updates the subscribers to that edition.

See also *edition* and *publisher* in the Glossary and *Automatic Updating* in the Command Reference.

suitcase

An icon that resembles a suitcase; a location where previous System versions stored fonts and desk accessories.

See also *Desk Accessories* and *Fonts* in the Command Reference.

System extension

A file, loaded when you start your Macintosh, that extends the capabilities of your computer by supporting printers, networks, or other features that are not part of the Macintosh itself.

See also *Extensions Folder* in the Command Reference.

System file

The file, contained in the System Folder, that tells your Macintosh how to display menus, what keyboard layout to use, what sound to play as the "beep," what fonts are available, and so on.

See also *System File* in the Command Reference.

System Folder

The folder that contains the software the Macintosh needs to operate properly. By convention, this folder is called the System Folder, but you can name the folder something else.

The Macintosh designates this folder as the "Blessed Folder" and displays a Macintosh icon inside the folder icon.

See also *System Folder* in the Command Reference.

System Software

The collective term for the System and Finder, as well as the desk accessories, fonts, startup documents, and so on that Apple supplies with your Macintosh.

thumb

The square box on a scroll bar that indicates your relative position in the window's contents.

See also *scroll bar*.

title bar

The striped bar at the top of the window (where the title of the window appears).

See also *Windows* in the Macintosh Basics section.

TrueType font

Also called an *outline font* or *variable-size font*. A font that the Macintosh can display accurately at any size.

See also *font* in the Glossary and *TrueType Fonts* in the Command Reference.

variable-size font

See *TrueType font*.

virtual memory

A feature of System 7 that enables you to use part of your Macintosh's hard drive as extra RAM.

See also *Memory Control Panel* and *Virtual Memory* in the Command Reference.

virus

A computer program that replicates itself, written with the intent of wreaking havoc within your computer.

window

An area on-screen that contains a document or other information. A window can consist of a title bar, scroll bars, close box, size box, and zoom box; however, not all windows have all features.

See also *Windows* in the Macintosh Basics section.

zoom box

The box you use to reduce or enlarge a window. The zoom box is the box within a box in the upper right corner of a window (at the right end of the title bar).

See also *Windows* in the Macintosh Basics section.

Index

Computer Books from Que Mean PC Performance!

Spreadsheets

1-2-3 Beyond the Basics	$24.95
1-2-3 Database Techniques	$29.95
1-2-3 for DOS Release 2.3 Quick Reference	$ 9.95
1-2-3 for DOS Release 2.3 QuickStart	$19.95
1-2-3 for Windows Quick Reference	$ 9.95
1-2-3 for Windows QuickStart	$19.95
1-2-3 Graphics Techniques	$24.95
1-2-3 Macro Library, 3rd Edition	$39.95
1-2-3 Release 2.2 PC Tutor	$39.95
1-2-3 Release 2.2 QueCards	$19.95
1-2-3 Release 2.2 Workbook and Disk	$29.95
1-2-3 Release 3 Workbook and Disk	$29.95
1-2-3 Release 3.1 Quick Reference	$ 8.95
1-2-3 Release 3.1 + QuickStart, 2nd Edition	$19.95
Excel for Windows Quick Reference	$ 9.95
Quattro Pro Quick Reference	$ 8.95
Quattro Pro 3 QuickStart	$19.95
Using 1-2-3/G	$29.95
Using 1-2-3 for DOS Release 2.3, Special Edition	$29.95
Using 1-2-3 for Windows	$29.95
Using 1-2-3 Release 3.1, + 2nd Edition	$29.95
Using Excel 3 for Windows, Special Edition	$29.95
Using Quattro Pro 3, Special Edition	$24.95
Using SuperCalc5, 2nd Edition	$29.95

Databases

dBASE III Plus Handbook, 2nd Edition	$24.95
dBASE IV PC Tutor	$29.95
dBASE IV Programming Techniques	$29.95
dBASE IV Quick Reference	$ 8.95
dBASE IV 1.1 QuickStart	$19.95
dBASE IV Workbook and Disk	$29.95
Que's Using FoxPro	$29.95
Using Clipper, 2nd Edition	$29.95
Using DataEase	$24.95
Using dBASE IV	$29.95
Using ORACLE	$29.95
Using Paradox 3	$24.95
Using PC-File	$24.95
Using R:BASE	$29.95

Business Applications

Allways Quick Reference	$ 8.95
Introduction to Business Software	$14.95
Introduction to Personal Computers	$19.95
Norton Utilities Quick Reference	$ 8.95
PC Tools Quick Reference, 2nd Edition	$ 8.95
Q&A Quick Reference	$ 8.95
Que's Computer User's Dictionary, 2nd Edition	$10.95
Que's Using Enable	$29.95
Que's Wizard Book	$12.95
Quicken Quick Reference	$ 8.95
SmartWare Tips, Tricks, and Traps, 2nd Edition	$26.95
Using DacEasy, 2nd Edition	$24.95
Using Managing Your Money, 2nd Edition	$19.95
Using Microsoft Works: IBM Version	$22.95
Using Norton Utilities	$24.95
Using PC Tools Deluxe	$24.95
Using Peachtree	$27.95
Using ProCOMM PLUS, 2nd Edition	$24.95
Using Q&A 4	$27.95
Using Quicken: IBM Version, 2nd Edition	$19.95
Using SmartWare II	$29.95
Using Symphony, Special Edition	$29.95
Using TimeLine	$24.95
Using TimeSlips	$24.95

CAD

AutoCAD Quick Reference	$ 8.95
Que's Using Generic CADD	$29.95
Using AutoCAD, 3rd Edition	$29.95
Using Generic CADD	$24.95

Word Processing

Microsoft Word Quick Reference	$ 9.95
Using LetterPerfect	$22.95
Using Microsoft Word 5.5: IBM Version, 2nd Edition	$24.95
Using MultiMate	$24.95
Using PC-Write	$22.95
Using Professional Write	$22.95
Using Word for Windows	$24.95
Using WordPerfect 5	$27.95
Using WordPerfect 5.1, Special Edition	$27.95
Using WordStar, 3rd Edition	$27.95
WordPerfect PC Tutor	$39.95
WordPerfect Power Pack	$39.95
WordPerfect 5 Workbook and Disk	$29.95
WordPerfect 5.1 QueCards	$19.95
WordPerfect 5.1 Quick Reference	$ 8.95
WordPerfect 5.1 QuickStart	$19.95
WordPerfect 5.1 Tips, Tricks, and Traps	$24.95
WordPerfect 5.1 Workbook and Disk	$29.95

Hardware/Systems

DOS Tips, Tricks, and Traps	$24.95
DOS Workbook and Disk, 2nd Edition	$29.95
Fastback Quick Reference	$ 8.95
Hard Disk Quick Reference	$ 8.95
MS-DOS PC Tutor	$39.95
MS-DOS 5 Quick Reference	$ 9.95
MS-DOS 5 QuickStart, 2nd Edition	$19.95
MS-DOS 5 User's Guide, Special Edition	$29.95
Networking Personal Computers, 3rd Edition	$24.95
Understanding UNIX: A Conceptual Guide, 2nd Edition	$21.95
Upgrading and Repairing PCs	$29.95
Using Microsoft Windows 3, 2nd Edition	$24.95
Using MS-DOS 5	$24.95
Using Novell NetWare	$29.95
Using OS/2	$29.95
Using PC DOS, 3rd Edition	$27.95
Using Prodigy	$19.95
Using UNIX	$29.95
Using Your Hard Disk	$29.95
Windows 3 Quick Reference	$ 8.95

Desktop Publishing/Graphics

CorelDRAW! Quick Reference	$ 8.95
Harvard Graphics Quick Reference	$ 8.95
Que's Using Ventura Publisher	$29.95
Using Animator	$24.95
Using DrawPerfect	$24.95
Using Harvard Graphics, 2nd Edition	$24.95
Using Freelance Plus	$24.95
Using PageMaker 4 for Windows	$29.95
Using PFS: First Publisher, 2nd Edition	$24.95
Using PowerPoint	$24.95
Using Publish It!	$24.95

Macintosh/Apple II

The Big Mac Book, 2nd Edition	$29.95
The Little Mac Book	$12.95
Que's Macintosh Multimedia Handbook	$24.95
Using AppleWorks, 3rd Edition	$24.95
Using Excel 3 for the Macintosh	$24.95
Using FileMaker	$24.95
Using MacDraw	$24.95
Using MacroMind Director	$29.95
Using MacWrite	$24.95
Using Microsoft Word 4: Macintosh Version	$24.95
Using Microsoft Works: Macintosh Version, 2nd Edition	$24.95
Using PageMaker: Macintosh Version, 2nd Edition	$24.95

Programming/Technical

C Programmer's Toolkit	$39.95
DOS Programmer's Reference, 2nd Edition	$29.95
Network Programming in C	$49.95
Oracle Programmer's Guide	$29.95
QuickC Programmer's Guide	$29.95
UNIX Programmer's Quick Reference	$ 8.95
UNIX Programmer's Reference	$29.95
UNIX Shell Commands Quick Reference	$ 8.95
Using Assembly Language, 2nd Edition	$29.95
Using BASIC	$24.95
Using Borland C++	$29.95
Using C	$29.95
Using QuickBASIC 4	$24.95
Using Turbo Pascal	$29.95

For More Information, Call Toll Free!

1-800-428-5331

All prices and titles subject to change without notice.
Non-U.S. prices may be higher.
Printed in the U.S.A.

Find It Fast With Que's Quick References!

Que's Quick References are the compact, easy-to-use guides to essential application information. Written for all users, Quick References include vital command information under easy-to-find alphabetical listings. Quick References are a must for anyone who needs command information fast!

1-2-3 for DOS Release 2.3 Quick Reference

Release 2.3

$9.95 USA
0-88022-725-7, 160 pp., 4 ¾ x 8

1-2-3 Release 3.1 Quick Reference

Releases 3 & 3.1

$8.95 USA
0-88022-656-0, 160 pp., 4 ¾ x 8

Allways Quick Reference

Version 1.0

$8.95 USA
0-88022-605-6, 160 pp., 4 ¾ x 8

AutoCAD Quick Reference, 2nd Edition

Releases 10 & 11

$8.95 USA
0-88022-622-6, 160 pp., 4 ¾ x 8

Batch File and Macros Quick Reference

Through DOS 5

$9.95 USA
0-88022-699-4, 160 pp., 4 ¾ x 8

CorelDRAW! Quick Reference

Through Version 2.01

$8.95 USA
0-88022-597-1, 160 pp., 4 ¾ x 8

dBASE IV Quick Reference

Version 1

$8.95 USA
0-88022-371-5, 160 pp., 4 ¾ x 8

Excel for Windows Quick Reference

Excel 3 for Windows

$9.95 USA
0-88022-722-2, 160 pp., 4 ¾ x 8

Fastback Quick Reference

Version 2.1

$8.95 USA
0-88022-650-1, 160 pp., 4 ¾ x 8

Hard Disk Quick Reference

Through DOS 4.01

$8.95 USA
0-88022-443-6, 160.pp., 4 ¾ x 8

Harvard Graphics Quick Reference

Version 2.3

$8.95 USA
0-88022-538-6, 160 pp., 4 ¾ x 8

Laplink Quick Reference

Laplink III

$9.95 USA
0-88022-702-8, 160 pp., 4 ¾ x 8

Microsoft Word Quick Reference

Through Version 5.5

$9.95 USA
0-88022-720-6, 160 pp., 4 ¾ x 8

Microsoft Works Quick Reference

Through IBM Version 2.0

$9.95 USA
0-88022-694-3, 160 pp., 4 ¾ x 8

MS-DOS 5 Quick Reference

Version 5

$9.95 USA
0-88022-646-3, 160 pp., 4 ¾ x 8

MS-DOS Quick Reference

Through Version 3.3

$8.95 USA
0-88022-369-3, 160 pp., 4 ¾ x 8

Norton Utilities Quick Reference

Norton Utilities 5 & Norton Commander 3

$8.95 USA
0-88022-508-4, 160 pp., 4 ¾ x 8

PC Tools 7 Quick Reference

Through Version 7

$9.95 USA
0-88022-829-6, 160 pp., 4 ¾ x 8

Q&A 4 Quick Reference

Versions 2, 3, & 4

$9.95 USA
0-88022-828-8, 160 pp., 4 ¾ x 8

Quattro Pro Quick Reference

Through Version 3

$8.95 USA
0-88022-692-7, 160 pp., 4 ¾ x 8

Quicken Quick Reference

IBM Through Version 4

$8.95 USA
0-88022-598-X, 160 pp., 4 ¾ x 8

UNIX Programmer's Quick Reference

AT&T System V, Release 3

$8.95 USA
0-88022-535-1, 160 pp., 4 ¾ x 8

UNIX Shell Commands Quick Reference

AT&T System V, Releases 3 & 4

$8.95 USA
0-88022-572-6, 160 pp., 4 ¾ x 8

Windows 3 Quick Reference

Version 3

$8.95 USA
0-88022-631-5, 160 pp., 4 ¾ x 8

WordPerfect 5.1 Quick Reference

WordPerfect 5.1

$8.95 USA
0-88022-576-9, 160 pp., 4 ¾ x 8

WordPerfect Quick Reference

WordPerfect 5

$8.95 USA
0-88022-370-7, 160 pp., 4 ¾ x 8

To Order, Call:
(800) 428-5331 OR (317) 573-2500